ASTD Competency Study

MAPPING THE FUTURE

NEW WORKPLACE LEARNING AND PERFORMANCE COMPETENCIES

Paul R. Bernthal

Karen Colteryahn

Patty Davis

Jennifer Naughton

William J. Rothwell

Rich Wellins

Rothwell & Associates, Inc.

ASTD Press is an internationally renowned source of insightful and practical information on workplace learning and performance topics, including training basics, evaluation and return-on-investment (ROI), instructional systems development (ISD), e-learning, leadership, and career development.

Ordering information: Books published by ASTD Press can be purchased by visiting our website at store.astd.org or by calling 800.628.2783 or 703.683.8100.

Library of Congress Control Number: 2004092794

ISBN-10: 1-56286-368-1
ISBN-13: 978-1-56286-368-5

Acquisitions and Development Editor: Mark Morrow
Copyeditor: Kris Patenaude
Interior Design and Production: Kathleen Schaner
Cover Design: Charlene Osman
Cover Illustration: Michael Gushock

Printed by Victor Graphics Inc., Baltimore, Maryland. www.victorgraphics.com.

Table of Contents

Foreword

To ASTD Members and the Profession

For the past 20 years, ASTD has created competency models that define standards of excellence for the profession as it has grown and assimilated new thinking and practice. Each ASTD competency model marks a milestone in the expansion of the field from a singular focus on training to human and organization development to workplace learning and performance. The *ASTD 2004 Competency Study: Mapping the Future* is another milestone on that journey. It details the competencies that learning professionals need today and will need in the future.

Your role as a business professional has never been more critical. Your work must have a direct link to the goals and strategies of the business within which you operate. To get that elusive "seat" at the leadership table and remain relevant in your organization, you must constantly reinvent yourself. As a learning and performance professional, you are more than a developer of people; you are an enabler of outcomes and instruments for change. You help individuals grow, learn, and realize potential that, in turn, helps organizations perform at a higher level. The importance of your work stretches beyond individuals and organizations, beyond economies, and beyond cultures and borders.

As a member of the learning and performance field, you can use this competency model as a foundation for career growth and a map for future development. And by continually investing in your own development and growth, you will be a model for continuous learning and be able to provide increasingly higher levels of expertise to your customers, clients, and colleagues.

Through your skills and capabilities, the learning and performance profession has the potential to grow far beyond our expectations today. I invite you to continue the journey with ASTD.

John W. Coné
Consultant in Corporate Learning

Preface

Why Now?

To keep pace with changes, ASTD commissioned the *ASTD Competency Study: Mapping the Future.* This report contains the findings of that study.

As an association devoted to linking people, learning, and performance, ASTD has, as one of its top priorities, a commitment to serve its members and the profession by leading the way. The study aimed to accomplish that goal by providing a roadmap to guide those who enter the field, make hiring decisions, create curricula, and pursue diverse paths for professional development. To that end, ASTD selected Development Dimensions International (DDI), a global human resource consulting firm, and Rothwell & Associates (R&A), a consulting company that specializes in succession management and competency modeling, to conduct the study. We chose this team as partners because of their experience in competency modeling, their combined academic and business perspectives, and their long histories in the learning and performance industry.

This report contains rich information that serves many purposes. It identifies current and emerging trends and presents the new competency model for the profession. This model looks more to the future and is more strategic than those from previous years, enabling individuals and institutions to remain ahead of the curve and equipping them to better align with organizational priorities. Additionally, it provides a comprehensive view of the field that, ultimately, will provide the foundation for the development of competency-based applications and learning tools that people can really use.

Further, the model provides an architecture and common frame of reference. Specifically, it provides a coherent picture to help unify the profession and reduce the fragmentation that exists in the field. It provides a means to define the various professional areas of expertise and to describe how the field is advancing and evolving. It also provides the raw materials for individuals and organizations to identify which competencies they will need for success.

Now is the most exciting and intense time in the history of the workforce learning and performance profession. This is a convergence point—one that offers limitless possibilities to mobilize and transform potential into tangible gains. To a great extent, workplace learning and performance professionals are already in a powerful position because they influence what people think and learn every day. But, the profession also must strive to embrace the future and make an even greater difference—one that will have an enduring impact in years to come. We urge you to heed the call—to use the information in this report wisely and to play an active role in shaping the future of the profession.

On behalf of ASTD, we are pleased to present the findings from the ASTD workplace learning and performance competency study.

Jennifer Naughton
ASTD Competency
   Study Manager
JNaughton@astd.org

Tony Bingham
ASTD President
   and CEO
Tony@astd.org

About the Sponsors

ASTD

ASTD is a leading association of workplace learning and performance professionals, forming a world-class community of practice. ASTD's 70,000 members and associates come from more than 100 countries and thousands of organizations—multinational corporations, medium-size and small businesses, government, academia, consulting firms, and product and service suppliers. ASTD marked its beginning in 1944 when the organization held its first annual conference. In recent years, it has widened the industry's focus to connect learning and performance to measurable results. ASTD is a sought-after voice on critical public policy issues. For more information, visit www.astd.org.

DDI

Since 1970, Development Dimensions International (DDI) has worked with some of the world's most successful organizations to achieve superior business results by building engaged, high-performing workforces. With 75 offices in 26 countries, DDI excels in two major areas: designing and implementing selection systems that enable organizations to hire better people faster, and identifying and developing exceptional leadership talent crucial to creating a workforce that drives sustainable success. To learn more, visit www.ddiworld.com.

Rothwell & Associates

Rothwell & Associates Inc. is a consulting company that specializes in succession management and competency modeling. It has served more than 35 multinational corporations. Recent works published by Rothwell & Associates Inc. include a study of learning competencies and organizational learning climate (*The Workplace Learner*, AMACOM, 2002), CEO perceptions of trainers' competencies (*What CEOs Expect from Corporate Training*, AMACOM, 2003), and a book about reinventing the HR function around competencies (*Competency-Based Human Resource Management*, Davies-Black, 2004). To learn more, visit www.rothwell-associates.com. See also www.ed.psu.edu/wfed.

About the Authors

Paul R. Bernthal

Paul R. Bernthal is the manager of DDI's Center for Applied Behavioral Research (CABER), where he works with internal and external clients to conduct benchmarking research, implement evaluation and validation research designs, and provide ongoing measurement consulting. He manages all of DDI's research activities and is an expert in evaluation, validation, and survey methods. He has conducted more than 15 international surveys in areas such as job/role competencies, leader development, performance management, the globalization of HR, and high-performance work practices. Additionally, he has conducted competency validation studies, developed leadership training programs, and participated in the development of a wide variety of WLP-related programs. He regularly speaks at conferences, and his work has been published in books and journals such as *Advances in International Comparative Management, T+D,* and *Group and Organizational Behavior.* He holds a Ph.D. in social psychology from The University of North Carolina at Chapel Hill.

Karen Colteryahn

Karen Colteryahn is the manager of knowledge management for DDI, where she provides vision and direction for DDI's knowledge management initiatives and coordinates its total quality implementation. She has more than 20 years' experience in providing project leadership and process expertise for interventions requiring process redesign or major change. She serves as a consultant to internal and external clients in organizational change, continuous improvement, process reengineering, knowledge management, measurement, and benchmarking. In addition to receiving a master's degree in business administration from the University of South Florida, she has been recognized as a certified management consultant (CMC) by the Institute of Management Consultants and a certified customer service executive (CCSE) by the International Customer Service Association.

Patty Davis

Patty Davis served as the DDI project manager for the 2004 ASTD competency study. She is a senior consultant at DDI and has been with the organization for more than 18 years. Her responsibilities include managing large-scale HR system implementations, tailoring and customizing DDI solutions to meet client specifications, and providing consulting services for competency analysis projects. She also frequently leads senior-executive strategy and system-implementation planning sessions. She worked in DDI's United Kingdom office for two years and coordinated many global HR system interventions. She has published more than 15 articles and white papers, the most recent of which appeared in the January 2004 *T+D* entitled "8 Trends You Need to Know Now." She holds a master's degree in industrial psychology.

Jennifer Naughton

Jennifer Naughton joined ASTD in spring 2003 to manage the 2004 ASTD competency study. Previously, she was an HR consultant for Booz Allen Hamilton and a research scientist at the Human Resources Research Organization (HumRRO). She has more than 12 years' experience in the human resource and training fields, and she specializes in research and evaluation, large-scale data collection, job analysis and competency modeling, certification design and personnel selection, and human resource systems design. She has written more than 25 reports for government, association, and military clients during her tenure as a consultant. In 2001, she received the Al Gore Hammer Award from the National Partnership for Reinventing Government for her work on the IRS Modernization Design Project. She also has been recognized as a certified senior human resource professional (SPHR). She holds a master's degree in human resource development from George Washington University.

William J. Rothwell

William J. Rothwell is president of Rothwell & Associates Inc. In that capacity, he runs an HR consulting company that specializes in train-the-trainer consulting services as well as a full gamut of other HR-related consulting services. He also is professor-in-charge of workforce education and development at the University Park campus of Pennsylvania State University, where he heads a graduate program in workplace learning and performance. He was a researcher on the previous ASTD-sponsored competency studies, *ASTD Models for Workplace Learning and Performance: Roles, Competencies, and Outputs* (with Sanders & Soper, 1999) and *ASTD Models for Human Performance Improvement,* 2d ed. (2000) of which he also served as editor. He is the author, co-author, editor, and co-editor of more than 50 books. Some of his recent publications include *What CEOs Expect from Corporate Training* (with Lindholm & Wallick, 2003, AMACOM) and *The Workplace Learner: How to Align Training Initiatives with Individual Learning Competencies* (AMACOM, 2002). He received his doctorate with a specialty in employee training from the University of Illinois at Urbana-Champaign.

Rich Wellins

Rich Wellins is a senior vice president with DDI. His responsibilities include strategic planning, new product launches, and research and evaluation as well as managing DDI's alliance program. He is currently working on the development and launch of a new leadership development system and a number of new reports on leadership and future HR trends. He has written for more than 20 publications and published six books, including the best-seller *Empowered Teams* (Jossey-Bass, 1991), *Inside Teams* (Jossey-Bass, 1994), and *Reengineering's Missing Ingredient: The Human Factor* (Institute of Personnel and Development, 1994). He has made more than 100 presentations at professional conferences around the world. He received a doctorate in social/industrial psychology from American University in Washington, D.C.

2004 ASTD Competency Project Team

ASTD

Tony Bingham
President and CEO
ASTD
Alexandria, VA

John Coné
Consultant in Corporate Learning
Alexandria, VA

Pat Galagan
Managing Director of Content
ASTD
Alexandria, VA

Jennifer Homer
Director of Public Relations
ASTD
Alexandria, VA

Jennifer Naughton
Competency Project Manager
ASTD
Alexandria, VA

Nancy Olson
Director of Education
ASTD
Alexandria, VA

DDI

Paul R. Bernthal
Manager
Center for Applied Behavioral
    Research (CABER)
DDI
Bridgeville, PA

Jason Bondra
Research Associate
Center for Applied Behavioral
    Research (CABER)
DDI
Bridgeville, PA

Bill Byham
Chairman and Chief Executive
    Officer
DDI
Bridgeville, PA

Karen Colteryahn
Manager
Knowledge Management
DDI
Bridgeville, PA

Patty Davis
DDI Competency Project
    Manager
Senior Consultant
DDI
Longboat Key, FL

Shawn Garry
Editor
DDI
Bridgeville, PA

Priscilla Kosarich
Administrative Assistant
DDI
Bridgeville, PA

Ann O'Shea
Senior Administrative Assistant
DDI
Bridgeville, PA

Tammy Pordash
Supervisor
Word Processing
DDI
Bridgeville, PA

Bill Proudfoot
Manager
Editorial
DDI
Bridgeville, PA

Rich Wellins
Senior Vice President of Global
    Marketing
DDI
Bridgeville, PA

Janet Wiard
Senior Graphic Designer
DDI
Bridgeville, PA

Rothwell & Associates

William J. Rothwell
President
Rothwell & Associates Inc.
State College, PA

Deborah Jo King Stern
Ph.D. Intern
Workforce Education and
    Development
College of Education,
    Department of Learning and
    Performance Systems
The Pennsylvania State University
University Park, PA

Advisory Committee

Katherine Holt
President
Peakinsight LLC
Durango, CO

Janis S. Houston
Principal Research Scientist
Personnel Decisions Research
  Institutes Inc.
Minneapolis, MN

Nancy Thomas
Director
The Chauncey Group
  International
a Division of Capstar
Princeton, NJ

Executive Summary

Having a defined set of competencies is a hallmark of a true profession, and the practice of creating and supporting a competency model is a key role of a professional association.

For the past 20 years, the American Society for Training & Development (ASTD) has created competency models that define standards of excellence for the profession as it has grown and assimilated new thinking and practice. Each ASTD competency model marks a milestone in the expansion of the field from a singular focus on training to human and organization development to workplace learning and performance. The *ASTD Competency Study: Mapping the Future* is another milestone on that journey. It provides a framework for the competencies that learning professionals need today and will need in the future.

The study culminated in this report, which contains a new competency model that defines the profession in the context of its strategic contribution to performance. It also addresses the need for the profession to balance its contribution to the organization's financial performance with the social well-being of people as they work.

The purpose of this report is to

- identify trends and drivers with the greatest impact on the current and future practice of the profession
- describe a competency model that is comprehensive, inspiring, and future-oriented
- provide a foundation for competency-based applications, deliverables, and outputs—including credentialing and follow-up research.

Eight Trends Shaping the Profession

This landmark report was created with the participation of more than 2,000 ASTD members and other practitioners who helped define the current and future state of the profession in the rapidly changing world of work. They also identified key trends—including economic, social, and technological—that are shaping the profession. The following eight trends are driving change in the workplace and will have significant implications for workplace learning and performance (WLP) professionals.

1. Drastic Times, Drastic Measures

Uncertain economic conditions in recent years are causing organizations to rethink how to grow and be profitable. Worldwide fear of terrorism and the additional cost of security are affecting economic stability and financial markets. These unstable conditions will drive organizations to continue to improve efficiency, productivity, and service quality while controlling costs and using limited financial and human resources.

> *"Over the past decade, the world (and especially the U.S. economy) has been focused on efficiency and effectiveness. It will take more focus on people and creativity to get organizations to the next level. Our profession is at risk if we don't learn how to help organizations create and innovate. Learning and performance professionals who do that will be the heroes. Right now, they are the pioneers."*
>
> Phil Harkins, CEO, Linkage

2. Blurred Lines—Life or Work?

New organizational structures are altering the nature of work for employees and learning professionals. Organizations are becoming more streamlined, flexible, networked, flat, diverse, and virtual—resulting in a blurring of lines between work and home, and where and when work occurs. Many people feel overworked and on call 24/7. Personal time constraints are raising stress levels and affecting the quality of family life. People want to be living while they're working, not just working for a living.

3. Small World and Shrinking

Global communication technology is changing the way people connect. The global economy is changing the nature of the marketplace and increasing interdependence and global competition. In addition, organizations are embracing offshore outsourcing as a way to stay competitive.

4. New Faces, New Expectations

Diversity in the workplace is on the rise. A more diverse workforce means accommodating new attitudes, lifestyles, values, and levels of motivation. Temporary workers will be used more often than in the past for specific tasks, and there will be greater demand for highly skilled workers. Increasing numbers of retirees could leave experience gaps in the workplace.

5. Work Be Nimble, Work Be Quick

The accelerated pace of change requires more adaptable workers and nimbler organizations. According to some sources, the estimated rate of change doubles every 10 years. Faster information processing and reduced cycle times ratchet up the pressure to work quickly.

6. Security Alert!

Concerns about both security and the effectiveness of governments to provide protection have increased people's anxiety worldwide. Organizations are increasingly concerned with the safety of the workforce and the security of their intellectual property.

7. Life and Work in the E-Lane

Technology, especially the Internet, is transforming the way people work and live. It has helped organizations achieve incredible efficiencies in many areas, including learning. It has accelerated the integration of learning and work and has reshaped thinking about when and where learning may occur.

8. A Higher Ethical Bar

Ethical lapses at the highest levels in large, high-profile organizations have shaken employees' loyalty, trust, and sense of security. Employees now question the integrity of leaders and the value of leadership development. They look harder at an organization's values.

> In DDI's 2003–2004 Leadership Forecast: a Benchmarking Study report, for which 1,600 leaders worldwide were surveyed, 57 percent said they're paying more attention to the ethics of their immediate managers and supervisors.

The Implications

In the ever-changing workplace, where escalating performance requirements make the learning professional's role more critical, there are a number of lessons to draw from current trends:

- *Know, grow, and speak the business.* It's no longer enough to be expert at learning and development theory and implementation. Today's WLP practitioners need to understand an organization's goals and align learning and development strategies and performance interventions with them.
- *Show them the value.* WLP professionals must demonstrate a payback from their efforts in the form of improved organizational performance

> "ROI analyses may not always be practical, but it is critical for practitioners to ensure their initiatives are producing expected changes in people performance and, ultimately, in the business."
>
> Bill Byham, founder, chairman, and CEO, DDI

and measurable results. The focus is on improving results and making a positive impact on business performance.

- *Make sure the high road starts here.* Help the organization develop a culture of integrity that is worthy of—and builds—employee trust. Support the profession's integrity by honoring its commitment to the value of people in the workplace and to the importance of purpose and meaning in work.

- *Be tech savvy or be sorry.* Understand learning technology, its current applications, and its potential. Use it to enhance learning and performance and to bring flexibility, timeliness, and personalization to learning.

"We all need a basic knowledge of technology so that we can use it to its best advantage. We need to learn how to blend different modalities of technology....We need to break our complacency and move fast. We need to be bold and take risks and have a bias for action...."

Kevin Oakes, chairman and CEO, Click2learn

- *Weave a world-wise Web.* Understand and respond to the reality of globalization and its diversity of learning and communication styles. Consider using new technologies to engage employees across the globe in learning and to keep them connected to organizational goals.

- *Be a talent purveyor: scout, agent, coach, and champion.* Play a role in determining what kind of talent organizations need to meet their goals, and then devise development and retention strategies to meet that need. Select appropriate talent, and

---

"Forward-thinking companies will increasingly start to position themselves to be attractive to the best people that they want to draw in—people who truly want to contribute to economic, social, and environmental well-being."

Peter Senge, author of *The Fifth Discipline* and founding chair of the Society for Organizational Learning

---

develop employees to become productive faster, to contribute more, and to stay longer.

A Model for Today and the Future

A model for this dynamic and complex profession must paint a picture of the current reality and also point toward the future; things are moving too fast to do otherwise. It must also encompass the sometimes conflicting perspectives of the pragmatic performance champions and those with their eyes on the long-term benefit for humankind.

This report paints a picture of what to expect over the next few years. It's an image that begs the need for a new competency model—a model that spells success for learning and performance practitioners now and in the years to come. Because the profession spans a range of expert areas of focus, the model (see figure 1) is broad enough to cover all WLP jobs, but it is not so broad that it can be applied to jobs outside the profession. It is also specific enough to outline real requirements for some jobs in the WLP profession.

This competency model also serves as an excellent resource for professional growth and development. It is comprehensive enough to guide career development at all levels of the profession, and it covers a wider spectrum of roles than any previous ASTD model.

The model includes three layers of knowledge and skill areas: competencies, areas of professional expertise, and roles.

Competencies

Competencies encompass the clusters of skills, knowledge, abilities, and behaviors required for success across all WLP jobs. Competencies anchor the model because they are foundational in nature. Job success will be difficult to achieve without some level of expertise in the majority of these competencies. Each competency includes a definition and list of key actions important for success (see appendix A). The model divides the foundational competencies into three clusters: Interpersonal, Business/Management, and Personal (see figure 2). Following are definitions of those competencies.

Figure 1. 2004 ASTD competency model.

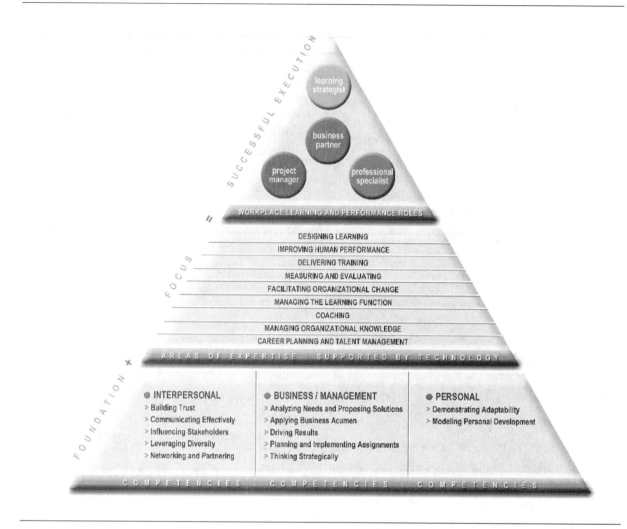

Figure 2. Foundational competencies.

Interpersonal Competencies

- *Building Trust*—Interacting with others in a way that gives them confidence in one's intentions and those of the organization.
- *Communicating Effectively*—Expressing thoughts, feelings, and ideas in a clear, concise, and compelling manner in both individual and group situations; actively listening to others; adjusting style to capture the attention of the audience; developing and deploying targeted communication strategies that inform and build support.
- *Influencing Stakeholders*—Selling the value of learning or the recommended solution as a way of improving organizational performance; gaining commitment to solutions that will improve individual, team, and organizational performance.
- *Leveraging Diversity*—Appreciating and leveraging the capabilities, insights, and ideas of all individuals; working effectively with individuals having diverse styles, abilities, motivations, and backgrounds (including cultural differences).
- *Networking and Partnering*—Developing and using a network of collaborative relationships with internal and external contacts to leverage the workplace learning and performance strategy in a way that facilitates the accomplishment of business results.

Business/Management Competencies

- *Analyzing Needs and Proposing Solutions*—Identifying and understanding business issues and client needs, problems, and opportunities; comparing data from different sources to draw conclusions; using effective approaches for choosing a course of action or developing appropriate solutions; taking action that is consistent with available facts, constraints, and probable consequences.
- *Applying Business Acumen*—Understanding the organization's business model and financial goals; utilizing economic, financial, and organizational data to build and document the business case for investing in workplace learning and performance solutions; using business terminology when communicating with others.
- *Driving Results*—Identifying opportunities for improvement and setting well-defined goals related to learning and performance solutions; orchestrating efforts and measuring progress; striving to achieve goals and produce exceptional results.
- *Planning and Implementing Assignments*—Developing action plans, obtaining resources, and completing assignments in a timely manner to ensure that workplace learning and performance goals are achieved.
- *Thinking Strategically*—Understanding internal and external factors that affect learning and performance in organizations; keeping abreast of trends and anticipating opportunities to add value to the business; operating from a systems perspective in developing learning and performance strategies and building alignment with business strategies.

Personal Competencies

- *Demonstrating Adaptability*—Maintaining effectiveness when experiencing major changes in work tasks, the work environment, or conditions affecting the organization (for example, economic, political, cultural, or technological); remaining open to new people, thoughts, and approaches; adjusting effectively to work within new work structures, processes, requirements, or cultures.
- *Modeling Personal Development*—Actively identifying new areas for one's own personal learning; regularly creating and taking advantage of learning opportunities; applying newly gained knowledge and skill on the job.

Areas of Expertise

Areas of expertise (AOEs) are the specific technical and professional skills and knowledge required for success in WLP specialty areas (see figure 3). Although some WLP professionals are highly specialized, most demonstrate expertise in more than one AOE. The AOEs are positioned above competencies on the model graphic because they direct and supplement the competencies through specialized skills and knowledge. All the AOEs rely on specialized technologies, such as Web-based training, automated evaluations, or online coaching, to leverage and support their skill or knowledge. Each AOE in the model includes a definition, a list of key actions, and a list of key knowledge areas (see appendix A). Following are definitions of the AOEs in the model.

- *Career Planning and Talent Management*— Ensuring that employees have the right skills to meet the strategic challenges of the organization; ensuring the alignment of individual career planning and organization talent management processes to achieve an optimal match between individual and organizational needs; promoting individual growth and organizational renewal.

- *Coaching*—Using an interactive process to help individuals and organizations develop more rapidly and produce more satisfying results; improving others' ability to set goals, take action, make better decisions, and make full use of their natural strengths.

- *Delivering Training*—Delivering learning solutions (for example, courses, guided experience) in a manner that both engages the learner and produces desired outcomes; managing and responding to learner needs; ensuring that the learning solution is made available or delivered in a timely and effective manner.

- *Designing Learning*—Designing, creating, and developing learning interventions to meet needs; analyzing and selecting the most appropriate strategy, methodologies, and technologies to maximize the learning experience and impact.

- *Facilitating Organizational Change*—Leading, managing, and facilitating change within organizations.

- *Improving Human Performance*—Applying a systematic process of discovering and analyzing human performance gaps; planning for future improvements in human performance; designing and developing cost-effective and ethically justifiable solutions to close performance gaps; partnering with the customer when identifying the opportunity and the solution; implementing the solution; monitoring the change; evaluating the results.

- *Managing Organizational Knowledge*—Serving as a catalyst and visionary for knowledge sharing; developing and championing a plan for transforming the organization into a knowledge-creating and knowledge-sharing entity; initiating, driving, and integrating the organization's knowledge management efforts.

- *Managing the Learning Function*—Providing leadership in developing human capital to execute the organization's strategy; planning, organizing, monitoring, and adjusting activities associated with the administration of workplace learning and performance.

- *Measuring and Evaluating*—Gathering data to answer specific questions regarding the value or impact of learning and performance solutions; focusing on the impact of individual programs and creating overall measures of system effectiveness; leveraging findings to increase effectiveness and provide recommendations for change.

The Influence of Technology

Learning technologies have had a profound influence on the evolution of the WLP profession. Knowledge of learning technologies and skill in their application are

Figure 3. Areas of expertise.

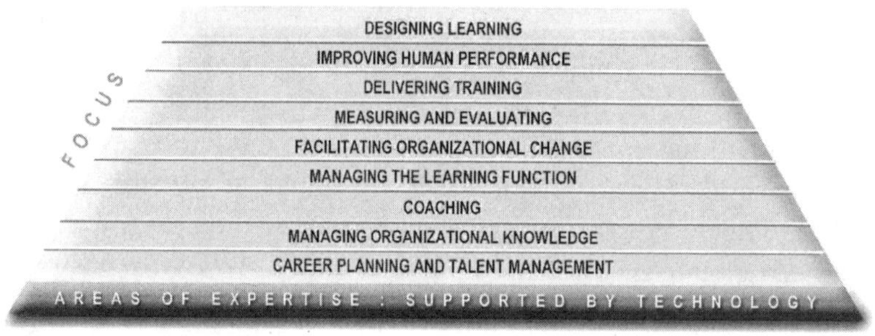

DESIGNING LEARNING
IMPROVING HUMAN PERFORMANCE
DELIVERING TRAINING
MEASURING AND EVALUATING
FACILITATING ORGANIZATIONAL CHANGE
MANAGING THE LEARNING FUNCTION
COACHING
MANAGING ORGANIZATIONAL KNOWLEDGE
CAREER PLANNING AND TALENT MANAGEMENT
FOCUS
AREAS OF EXPERTISE · SUPPORTED BY TECHNOLOGY

critical in many jobs and roles in the profession, but do not constitute discrete areas of expertise. Instead, they enable new forms of delivery and new ways of using learning to achieve performance. As such, they are imbedded in the key knowledge and key action areas that further define the AOEs (see appendix A).

Roles

Roles are broad areas of responsibility within the WLP profession that require a certain combination of competencies and AOEs to perform effectively. They are described in sensible, intuitive, and everyday language. Like competencies, roles can be demonstrated in the context of most WLP jobs. Roles are not the same as job titles; they are much more fluid, depending on the application or the project. For the WLP professional, playing the roles is analogous to maintaining a collection of hats—when the situation calls for it, the professional slips out of one role and "puts on" another. Roles occupy the peak of the model (see figure 4), because a vast body of underlying skills and knowledge supports their execution.

Four WLP Roles

- *Learning Strategist*—Determines how workplace learning and performance improvement can best be leveraged to achieve long-term business success and add value to meet organizational needs; leads in the planning and implementation of learning and performance improvement strategies that

support the organization's strategic direction and that are based on an analysis of the effectiveness of existing learning and performance-improvement strategies.

- *Business Partner*—Applies business and industry knowledge to partner with the client in identifying workplace performance-improvement opportunities; evaluates possible solutions and recommends solutions that will have a positive impact on performance; gains client agreement and commitment to the proposed solutions and collaboratively develops an overall implementation strategy that includes evaluating impact on business performance; uses appropriate interpersonal styles and communication methods to build effective long-term relationships with the client.
- *Project Manager*—Plans, resources, and monitors the effective delivery of learning and performance solutions in a way that supports the overall business venture; communicates purpose, ensures effective execution of an implementation plan, removes barriers, ensures adequate support, and follows up.
- *Professional Specialist*—Designs, develops, delivers, or evaluates learning and performance solutions; maintains and applies an in-depth working knowledge in any one or more of the workplace learning and performance specialty areas of expertise—Career Planning and Talent Management, Coaching, Delivering Training, Designing Learning, Facilitating Organizational Change,

Figure 4. WLP roles.

Improving Human Performance, Managing Organizational Knowledge, Managing the Learning Function, and Measuring and Evaluating.

Reinventing the "Wheel"

Past ASTD competency studies have used a "wheel" graphic to represent how WLP fits into the larger picture of human resource management and other areas of organizational operations. Figure 5 depicts an updated version of that wheel.

The purpose of the wheel is to

- show what disciplines typically might be considered part of the WLP profession
- help define the WLP profession in relation to traditional HR disciplines.

At the hub is business strategy. Because all the traditional HR and organizational disciplines and AOEs making up the "spokes" contribute to an organization's success, they must be aligned with the business strategy. This alignment drives and contributes to business performance.

The left side of the wheel shows the AOEs, which represent the WLP professional disciplines. The bottom left portion highlights AOEs that focus primarily on learning and development solutions as the means to improving performance. Meanwhile, the upper left portion represents AOEs that are broader in focus and that might include solutions other than learning and development interventions. For example, a WLP professional who is facilitating organizational change might be operating in the context of an organization's need to

Figure 5. Driving business performance.

restructure and change certain jobs. A professional who is expert in improving human performance might choose compensation and rewards and recognition as the primary solutions for improving performance.

Traditional HR disciplines appear in the upper right section of the wheel. Some of these include compensation and benefits as well as selection, staffing, and job design. The bottom right portion includes examples of other non-WLP or HR-related organizational functions, such as sales, marketing, and customer services.

All organizational disciplines help drive business performance. As the WLP profession continues to evolve, practitioners will more likely begin to incorporate solutions from other organizational disciplines to help them maximize their contributions.

The Proof Is in the Application

The competencies, AOEs, and roles defined in this report pinpoint the behaviors, knowledge, and responsibilities that are critical for workplace learning and performance professionals. The real value of the WLP competencies and AOEs is realized in their applica-

tion. WLP professionals need to work within their organizations to incorporate the roles, competencies, and AOEs into their own human resource systems to

- attract people into the profession
- evaluate individuals for selection or promotion
- diagnose training and development needs
- design training and development programs
- guide career-planning decisions
- guide coaching and feedback
- assess job performance
- establish a foundation for credentialing programs.

The competencies and AOEs also serve as a framework on which to organize WLP human resource systems. Figure 6 depicts some of the HR systems that can be built around competencies and AOEs.

For example, a WLP hiring manager can use the competencies and AOEs to select new employees who demonstrate the desired competencies and professional expertise. The same list of competencies and areas of expertise can be used in a performance management

Figure 6. HR systems that can be built around competencies and AOEs.

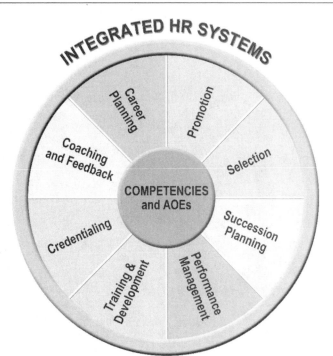

system to monitor and evaluate performance on the job. When employees need to improve their performance, the competencies can serve as the basis for choosing appropriate training and development activities.

The Mission

The WLP profession has always championed continuous learning and self-development as an indispensable part of the adult work experience. The ASTD Competency Model provides a blueprint for professionals to model continuous learning. By embracing learning and investing in personal development and growth, they will move the profession to higher levels of expertise and respect, and ensure competent service to customers, clients, and colleagues.

Introduction

A Strategic Roadmap for Professional Development

Ongoing and unrelenting economic, social, and technological changes have spurred the need for flexible, skilled workers who can help their organizations succeed and sustain a competitive advantage. To be relevant within organizations and indispensable to clients and customers alike, workplace learning and performance (WLP) professionals must continually reassess their competencies, update their skills, and have the courage to make necessary changes.

As an association devoted to linking people, learning, and performance, the American Society for Training & Development (ASTD) recognizes that its most critical priorities are to paint a clear picture of the profession, to position the profession for maximum success and impact, and to provide a strategic roadmap for professional development. To answer the call—and to keep pace with an ever-changing field—ASTD commissioned the *ASTD Competency Study: Mapping the Future.* This report is the culmination of that study. Building on ASTD's competency research from the past two decades as well as work from the team of Development Dimensions International (DDI) and Rothwell & Associates, this report will help guide the profession into the next generation.

This report contains a new competency model that defines the profession in the context of its strategic contribution to performance. It also addresses the need for the profession to balance its contribution to financial performance in organizations with the social well-being of people as they work. The report spans a wide range of professional levels—from those just entering the profession to those with many years of experience working at a very senior level—and includes international input. The purpose of the report is to

- identify trends and drivers with the greatest impact on the current and future practice of the profession
- describe a competency model that is comprehensive, inspiring, and future-oriented
- provide a foundation for competency-based applications, deliverables, and outputs—including credentialing for practitioners and follow-up research.

By clearly defining the workplace roles, current and emerging competencies, and areas of expertise needed to succeed, ASTD is confident that the findings in this report will support the needs of those interested and vested in the WLP profession.

Methodology Overview

To create the ASTD Competency Model, analysts began with three primary sources of data and progressed through an extensive review and validation process. Figure I-1 outlines the basic development process. A complete explanation of this process is included in appendix C.

During Phases I and II, content was drawn from a review of past ASTD studies, more than 100 articles, competency research studies, and more than 100 subject matter experts (see appendix E for a complete list of the individuals who contributed to this study). In Phase III, more than 2,000 WLP professionals rated the competencies, areas of expertise (AOEs), and roles in terms of importance for effectiveness in their current jobs. Most ratings were made using a 5-point scale:

1 = Unnecessary
2 = Slightly Important
3 = Moderately Important
4 = Very Important
5 = Essential.

Respondents rated 269 individual key actions and knowledge areas across all competencies, AOEs, and

Figure I-1. Process used to create the ASTD Competency Model.

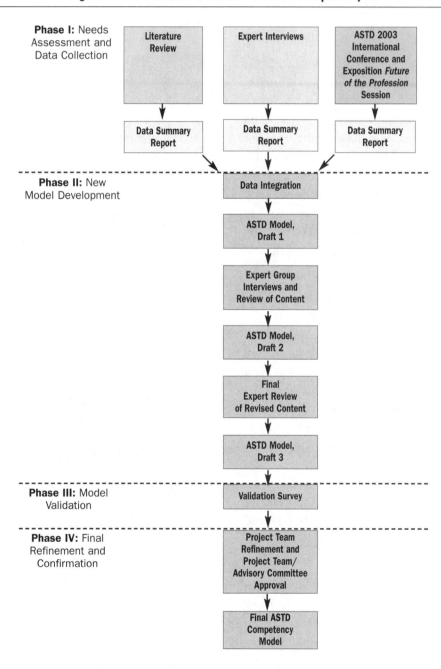

roles. Analysts set a minimum importance score of 3.5 as the criteria for including specific skills and knowledge areas in the model. Of the 269 skills and knowledge areas, less than 3 percent received ratings of under 3.5. Thus, it appears that nearly every component of this model is more than moderately important for a large number of WLP professionals.

In this report, the authors have attempted to balance readability with scientific detail. The executive summary covers the high-level findings and trends. Extensive detail about survey ratings, averages, and frequencies can be found in appendix D.

Other organizations and associations around the world have completed excellent studies about WLP competencies. In global applications, it is recommended to use those studies in conjunction with this report to gain a broader understanding of the WLP profession in other countries and cultures.

What You'll Find in This Report

The main body of this report contains seven chapters. Chapter 1 discusses important trends facing the WLP profession in the coming years. It is followed by a description of the ASTD Competency Model (chapter 2). Chapters 3 through 5 examine the model components—competencies, AOEs, and roles—drilling down to provide a complete explanation of each. Chapter 6 explains how the model can be applied by practitioners, both in business and education, and chapter 7 presents the conclusion and a call to action for WLP professionals.

The portion of the report beyond chapter 7 features four appendixes, including the competency dictionary (appendix A), a history of ASTD competency models (appendix B), the research methodology (appendix C), and the research summary with statistics (appendix D). Appendix E contains a listing of individuals and organizations—including ASTD chapters—contributing to the study. The five appendixes are followed by a reference section.

A CD-ROM is also provided with this book. The CD contains the competency dictionary (found in appendix A) and includes the definitions, key actions, and key knowledge areas that a WLP professional needs when creating a development plan.

Chapter 1

Eight Trends Shaping the Profession

....

The famed baseball player Yogi Berra once said "The future ain't what it used to be."

How right he was!

Change in the business world continues at an unprecedented rate, which, in turn, drives change in the workplace. The rate and depth of change mandate that workplace learning and performance (WLP) professionals rethink what they are doing now and what they should be doing in the future.

The competency study identified eight trends driving change in the workplace, plus significant implications that these trends have for WLP professionals. These trends and their implications were identified through:

- Interviews and focus groups with more than 100 thought leaders and practitioners in the learning and performance field, such as Warner Burke, Pat McLagan, Steve Piersanti, Jim Robinson, Allison Rossett, Peter Senge, and Meg Wheatley. (A complete list of the individuals who contributed to this study can be found in appendix E.)
- A review of numerous research studies and articles related to trends affecting the profession.
- Survey responses from more than 2,000 workplace learning and performance professionals—mostly ASTD HQ and chapter members.

Identifying trends and implications was an important part of the research project. The research team created a competency model that not only is appropriate today, but also will be relevant in the future. Identifying trends and their implications was a critical first step in developing a future-focused competency model that will enable practitioners to effect positive, progressive, and enduring change in organizations.

The Eight Trends

1. Drastic Times, Drastic Measures

Uncertain economic conditions in recent years are causing organizations to rethink how to grow and be profitable. Although no one has a crystal ball to predict future economic conditions precisely, a preponderance of data suggests that the U.S. economy will experience slow to moderate growth over the next few years. Worldwide fear of terrorism and the additional cost of high security are affecting economic stability and financial markets. Several sources indicate the likelihood of a prolonged labor shortage, meaning a return to a seller's market for talent. Those unstable conditions will drive organizations to continue looking to improve efficiency, productivity, and service quality while controlling costs and using limited financial and human resources.

In addition, there will be sharper focus on innovation as organizations redefine their business models. To grow, organizations must discover and enact new sources of value. That means a radical rethinking and doing more with less. Phil Harkins, CEO of Linkage, describes this shift: "Over the past decade, the world (and especially the U.S. economy) has been focused on efficiency and effectiveness. It will take more focus on people and creativity to get organizations to the next level. Our profession is at risk if we don't learn how to help organizations create and innovate. Learning and performance professionals who do that will be the heroes. Right now, they are the pioneers."

2. Blurred Lines—Life or Work?

New organizational structures are altering the nature of work for employees and learning professionals. Organizations continue to evolve in hopes of finding the most efficient structure for success in the volatile economic environment. They are becoming more streamlined, flexible, networked, flat, diverse, and virtual—blurring the lines between work and home, and where and when work occurs. More employees are telecommuting full- or part-time. Many people feel overworked and on call 24/7. The number of dual-earner families has increased. Personal time constraints are raising stress levels and affecting the quality of family life. People want to be living while they are working, not just working for a living.

Outsourcing is more commonplace for functions not considered core to the business. In some cases, that means human resource operations. British Petroleum is just one of hundreds of global corporations turning to business-process outsourcing, in which entire business functions—such as human resources, accounting, and claims processing—are outsourced. Similarly, some companies want to offload learning. According to Michael Brennan, corporate learning program manager for industry analyst IDC, corporate executives rate training as the function they'd most likely outsource in the next three to five years—ahead of sales and marketing, HR, finance, and accounting (Harris, 2003).

Another transformation is occurring in organizations that view outsourcing the learning and training function as a means to eliminate fixed costs, focus on core competencies, become more strategic, and contain the high and unpredictable costs of enterprise learning. A good case in point is Avaya University's relationship with Accenture, which provides outsourcing solutions for HR services. Accenture staffs and operates the university. Through Accenture's blended-learning solution, Avaya's classes have shifted from 80 percent

instructor-led to less than 50 percent. More than 200 Avaya employees were hired by Accenture to serve their former company and other clients (Harris, 2003).

3. Small World and Shrinking

Global communication technology is changing the way people connect. The global economy is altering the nature of the marketplace, promoting increased interdependence and worldwide competition. In addition, organizations are embracing offshore outsourcing as a way to stay competitive. Many functions are being shifted to India, the Philippines, Malaysia, Canada, Russia, and other countries for their lower labor costs and high workforce-education levels. According to the *2002–2003 SHRM Workplace Forecast*, corporations such as Ford, General Motors, and Nestlé employ more people outside than within the countries where their headquarters are located (Patel, 2002).

Almost any company, whether in manufacturing or services, can find some part of its work that can be done off site. Forrester Research projects that migration of service- and knowledge-based jobs will ship 3.3 million American jobs—70 percent of which will move to India—overseas by 2015 (Thottam, 2003). Communication and information sharing are occurring across the globe in many languages and cultures. Global competition is making way for global cooperation.

4. New Faces, New Expectations

Diversity in the workplace is on the rise. A more diverse workforce means new attitudes, lifestyles, values, and levels of motivation. According to a U.S. Census Bureau report published in June 2003, the Hispanic population increased by 9.8 percent between April 1, 2000, and July 1, 2002, making it the largest minority group in the United States (Bernstein and Bergman, 2003). In that same time period, the Asian population in the United States grew by about 9 percent, while the Caucasian population grew by 2 percent.

The population is growing at a high rate in developing countries, while remaining stable or decreasing in the developed world. This will continue to boost income inequities and economic opportunity, leading to increased immigration and migration within and between nations. More temporary workers will be used for specific tasks, and there will be a greater demand for highly skilled workers. Japan is a perfect example; its population is rapidly aging, and its birthrate is the lowest among industrialized nations. Japan's shrinking workforce will eventually lead it to accept large-scale immigration. According to *The New York Times* article, "Insular Japan Needs, but Resists, Immigration," a United Nations report recently forecast that to maintain the size of its working population, "Japan would need 17 million new immigrants by 2050" (French, 2003). This figure would represent 18 percent of the Japanese population compared with today's 1 percent.

The aging of the American workforce means more retirees and fewer experienced workers. According to the U.S. General Accounting Office (GAO), by 2015 nearly one in five U.S. workers will be age 55 or older (GAO, 2001). Retirees now often want to keep a foot in the workplace door. According to the American Association of Retired Persons (AARP), nearly eight of 10 baby boomers envision working at least part time during their retirement (Roper Starch Worldwide, 1999). Five percent anticipate working full time at a new job or career, while only 16 percent foresee not working at all. Europe's population is even older than that of the United States, and the age gap there is widening. In the United Kingdom, France, Germany, and Italy, 17-24 percent of the population is age 60 or older; by 2050, that percentage is projected to rise to 32-45 percent.

5. Work Be Nimble, Work Be Quick

The accelerated pace of change requires more adaptable workers and nimbler organizations. According to some sources, the rate of change doubles every 10 years, while the speed of information processing increases logarithmically. Research is beginning to identify the qualities of organizations capable of adapting quickly to change—whether to respond to opportunities or react to potential threats.

Recently, IBM built a $2.5 billion (U.S.) chip factory, which was designed for flexibility. It can adapt production to marketplace demand. With an eye toward on-demand computing, IBM has made a fundamental shift in its business strategy, requiring a nimble workforce and a leadership base equipped with the talent to train them. With its "The Role of the Manager@IBM"

program, IBM is combining e-learning, in-person workshops, and management communities in a four-tiered approach to address the individual, the team, and the organization (Galvin, Johnson, and Barbian, 2003).

Many organizations have been successful at reducing cycle times. Lockheed Martin Maritime Systems & Sensors in Syracuse, New York, reduced the cycle time for a ground-based radar system from 10 months to less than five months, while continuing a single-shift operation. The defense contractor accomplished a 41 percent increase in productivity through the use of Six Sigma quality principles, lean practices, and team-based problem solving (McClenahen, 2003). Also, Siemens AG's Computed Tomography division in Forchheim, Germany, implemented process improvement initiatives that shortened delivery time from 22 weeks to two weeks, cut processing times 76 percent, reduced inventory 40 percent, and improved delivery reliability from 80 percent to 99 percent (Drickhamer, 2002).

6. Security Alert!

Heightened security concerns are changing expectations for our personal lives and the role of organizations and governments. There's cynicism, pessimism, and anxiety about the future. The threat of terrorism worldwide has spiked organizations' concerns about the safety of their workforces and the security of their intellectual property. Employee monitoring and screening occur more frequently. Anxiety over traveling for business purposes is promoting alternative communication, such as teleconferencing, videoconferencing, and Web seminars.

People are looking to their governments and organizations to provide a safer work environment. Steve Piersanti, president of the Berrett-Koehler publishing firm, says, "More and more people are seeing that things are 'not OK' and are trying to change their lives. A growing number of people are questioning things—things that have yet to have an impact. We are in a new time, where there's a potential opening for rethinking things."

7. Life and Work in the E-Lane

Technology, especially the Internet, is transforming the way people work and live. Recent innovations have helped organizations achieve incredible market efficiencies in many areas, including learning. Technology also has accelerated the integration of learning and work and reshaped thinking about where and when learning may occur.

Email is faster and easier than traditional communication methods and now has language translation capability. Wireless technology allows text, video, pictures, and conversations to be shared at one's fingertips. For young people who will soon enter the workplace, technology is an extension of themselves.

8. A Higher Ethical Bar

Ethical lapses at the highest levels in large, high-profile organizations have shaken employees' loyalty, trust, and sense of security both in the United States and abroad. In 2003, business scandals involving WorldCom, Tyco, Adelphia, HealthSouth, Global Crossing, the New York Stock Exchange, Italian dairy giant Parmalat, Australia's HIH Insurance Group, and the Bank of China, to name a few, cast widespread doubt and fueled cynicism about corporate responsibility to the community and to the workforce.

Employees now question the integrity of leaders and the value of leadership development. They look harder at an organization's values. The level of trust in the workplace is at an all-time low. According to Development Dimensions International's 2003–2004 *Leadership Forecast: A Benchmarking Study* report, for which 1,600 leaders worldwide were surveyed, 57 percent of the leaders said they're paying more attention to the ethics of their immediate managers and supervisors (Bernthal and Wellins, 2003).

The Implications

In the ever-changing workplace, where escalating performance requirements make the learning professional's role more critical, there are a number of lessons related to the current trends.

Know, Grow, and Speak the Business

It's no longer enough to be expert at learning and development theory and implementation. Today's WLP practitioners need to understand their organiza-

tion's business goals and align learning and development strategies and performance interventions with them. Workplace learning and performance professionals need to understand where the business is heading. By anticipating the impact of the organizational strategy on the business and aligning interventions accordingly, practitioners will play a critical role in determining whether an organization is successful in achieving its goals.

A Business Understanding Checklist

How well do you understand your organization's business and strategies? Here are some ways to ensure your future success. Check all that represent areas of strength for you.

- ☐ Understand the organization's business, its business model, and how it makes money in its industry.
- ☐ Speak the language of the business to gain credibility.
- ☐ Understand financial statements and how they relate to business success measures.
- ☐ Provide advice on how human capital can be developed and aligned to meet current and future business needs.
- ☐ Recognize and act on emerging opportunities to quickly help prepare the workforce to respond to them.
- ☐ Understand what makes an organization a change- and learning-friendly environment and then support and develop that environment.
- ☐ Partner with senior leaders to establish learning and development strategies that support the organization's business strategy.

As Pat McLagan, president and CEO of the RITEstuff Inc. and McLagan International, says, "We need to sort out what's important from what's not. We need to know what problems to pay attention to and see what's important in the scheme of things, not just urgent. When HRD responds out of a sense of urgency, we can develop credibility as a reliable pair of hands. But that doesn't get us the seat at the table. We need to say, 'XYZ is happening and that has ABC impact on us short term and long term,' and then make a case for what to do. It's a proactive position based on big-picture and systemic thinking that we need in the long run."

For example, a key part of GM's global transformation involves developing HR people so that they understand

and can take on the role of internal consultants. Through mandatory coursework in business acumen, change management skills, and the ability to forge relationships across the organization, GM's HR personnel will be assisting business units that are having trouble achieving goals (Caudron, 2003).

Show Them the Value

WLP professionals must demonstrate a payback from their efforts in the form of improved organizational performance and measurable results. Their training, development, and other performance programs must improve results and make a positive impact on business performance. In the current economic environment, there are no employment guarantees—it is important to regularly prove one's value. According to the *2003 ASTD State of the Industry Report* (Thompson, et al., 2002), more organizations than ever before are conducting some kind of evaluation, and more are attempting higher levels of evaluation. Yet, only about one company in 10 is attempting any results-based,

Level 4 evaluation. (Level 4 evaluations measure how organizational outcomes—such as productivity, customer service, morale, efficiency, or profitability—have changed as a result of a training effort.)

Bill Byham, founder and CEO of Development Dimensions International (DDI), advises, "ROI analyses may not always be practical, but it is critical for practitioners to ensure their initiatives are producing expected changes in people performance and, ultimately, in the business."

Meanwhile, Jack Phillips, executive vice president of the Jack Phillips Center for Research, put it another way: "Today's metrics for learning and development must move beyond counting people, hours, programs, and smiles to include measures that reflect on-the-job application, business impact, and return-on-investment."

Make Sure the High Road Starts Here

Expectations have risen for ethical behavior and social responsibility in the workplace. Many practitioners view WLP as a "do-good" profession. They believe in a culture of trust, continued development, and ethical behavior. They also believe that WLP professionals can help organizations develop a culture of integrity that is worthy of—and builds—employee trust. By doing so, practitioners will support the integrity of the profession by honoring its commitment to the value of people in the workplace and to the importance of purpose and meaning in work.

A Business Performance Checklist

It's important that you can articulate the business value of your WLP initiatives. Check the items that represent strengths for you.

☐ Focus your efforts on improving areas that will enhance business performance, such as customer loyalty, product quality and innovation, speed of development and delivery, and sales effectiveness.

☐ Make sure there's a crystal-clear business case for an initiative (such as increased market share, improved leadership capability, reduction of key talent turnover) before any investment, including the identification of the initiative's drivers.

☐ Establish clear measures that help answer the questions "Why are we doing this in the first place?" "Have we been successful?" and "How will we know when we're successful?"

☐ Demonstrate return-on-investment (ROI) and business contribution by tying initiatives to lasting and important business metrics that are key differentiators, such as revenue, market share, quality, customer service and loyalty, retention, turnover, efficiency, and innovation.

☐ Communicate the results with those who matter, such as business partners and senior management.

An Ethics Checklist

Do you take the high road in the workplace? Check the items below that describe the actions you take to elevate integrity.

☐ Advocate and model organizational practices that respect the individual and support a humane workplace in times of instability and change.

☐ Value multidimensional learning experiences that facilitate the development of emotional and spiritual intelligence and knowledge and skills.

☐ Operate ethically and with integrity—"walk the talk."

☐ Lead by example and serve as a role model for the organization's values.

Margaret Wheatley, president of The Berkana Institute, encourages workplace learning and performance professionals to "go deeper into what we know, to move from certain tools and techniques to understanding the deeper wisdom of those processes. We should be much less dependent on techniques and more dependent on insight and clarity about human beings. That's asking a lot, but it's the work that needs to be done."

Cisco Systems is an example of an organization that has taken the high road, winning the 2003 Ron Brown Award, which recognizes companies for showing corporate leadership in cultivating outstanding community relations. Cisco won for an Internet-based program that trains students in 152 countries in Web technology, with a focus on developing countries. Fannie Mae also won the award for a program that its CEO Franklin Raines says helps retain employees. The program has lent 2,200 employees a 7 percent down payment on home purchases and forgiven the principal after five years (Conference Board, 2003).

Be Tech Savvy or Be Sorry

WLP professionals need to understand learning technology, its current applications, and its potential. They must be able to use it to develop and deliver training and learning more quickly and flexibly, in a variety of modalities, and at the moment of need. A combination of Web-based training with classroom instruction, knowledge management systems, email, videoconferences, guided chat rooms, and phone conferences can contribute to an effective learning strategy.

A Technologies Checklist

Which of the following statements describe your approach to linking training and technology? Check all that apply.

- ☐ Learn about new and emerging learning technologies and support systems and how they can best help deliver training and learning.

- ☐ Analyze and select training and learning technologies based on a needs-driven approach to meet diverse learner needs and accomplish learning goals and objectives.

- ☐ Integrate training and learning technology options to produce coherent blended-learning solutions that best meet an individual's learning needs and learning styles.

Some organizations are shifting from classroom training to other kinds of learning opportunities and just-in-time information that improves performance. Although there will continue to be a place for classroom training and organized training events, the new challenge is for WLP professionals to capture and catalog information, and enable learners to access it on demand.

According to Gloria Gery, of Gery Associates and a noted expert on e-learning, "We need to restructure knowledge resources and integrate them around work processes. Based on people's roles, we need to filter what they see, what they need to know, and what they do in their work processes."

Technology puts more information into the pipeline, but can cause information overload. Information needs to be analyzed, cataloged, and made accessible when needed. There are many ways that learning can and should be delivered, such as through colleagues, subject matter experts, managers, online learning communities of expertise, chat lines, and a variety of technology-based tools. The challenge is to provide a balance of alternatives that results in a flexible—yet efficient—learning environment.

For example, AmeriCredit modified its training to appeal to the learning styles of all employees and created a database to track each employee's learning style. More than 70 percent of the company's employees are in the database, and training facilitators are tailoring their sessions to reflect an awareness of each trainee's learning style (Galvin, Johnson, and Barbian, 2003).

Workplace learning and performance professionals may need to be re-skilled to understand the options available for achieving their organization's learning objectives. In some cases that might require them to undergo training on a host of HR technology products.

Kevin Oakes, chairman and CEO of Click2learn, advises, "The profession is not changing. Many of the things we knew we should be doing 10 years ago, but we're still not doing them. We all need a basic knowledge of technology so that we can use it to its best advantage. We need to learn how to blend different modalities of technology. We need Web-skilled instructional design. We need to break our complacency and move fast. We need to be bold and take risks and have a bias for action. Otherwise, this profession will continue to be an afterthought in most companies as opposed to what it can be: a mission-critical, strategic function."

Weave a World-Wise Web

Globalization is dramatically altering the face of business. Increasingly, as organizations move or expand their operations into other countries, WLP professionals must understand and respond to the reality of globalization and its diversity.

Organizations operating abroad might need to break out of their own paradigms and make a point to understand the cultural issues that could lead to low productivity and labor strife resulting from lack of motivation or alienation of culturally diverse populations.

A Diversity Checklist

Which of these actions do you take in responding to the issues of globalization and diversity? Check all that represent strengths for you.

☐ Understand cultural differences and how to develop, design, and implement training and learning solutions for a global, culturally diverse audience.

☐ Help your organization's leaders develop cultural sensitivities and abilities so that they can produce, market, and sell products and services in other cultures.

☐ Leverage diversity to help employees, including leaders, to understand and maximize relationships with associates from other cultures, countries, races, and backgrounds.

☐ Make your learning community and learning resources available worldwide.

Technology makes it possible for companies to become more decentralized, with employees distributed across wider geographic regions. As managing projects in multiple locations becomes more common, WLP professionals face diverse learning and communication styles, using new and different technologies.

Learning and performance consultants must be able to determine what training opportunities will best engage employees in locations across the globe. A bigger challenge is determining how to keep widely dispersed employees connected to organizational goals.

Be a Talent Purveyor: Scout, Agent, Coach, and Champion

Demographic changes are making it increasingly hard for organizations to find and keep qualified employees. Workplace learning and performance professionals must position themselves to play a critical role in determining what kind of talent is needed to meet organizational goals and then devise development and retention strategies to meet that need.

Though the soft U.S. job market of the past few years might be masking the impact of the coming talent shortage, the need to proactively manage and retain talent is more important than ever. The cost of recruiting, training, and bringing new talent on board is high. Therefore, developing strategies for retaining and developing existing talent is paramount. To build organizational capability, WLP professionals need to be helping their organizations select appropriate talent and develop employees to become productive faster, contribute more, and stay longer.

A Strategic Talent Checklist

How strong a part do you play in helping your organization select, develop, and retain talent? Check all that represent strengths for you.

☐ Ensure that employees have the right skills to meet the strategic challenges of the organization.

☐ Work with senior management to identify high-potential individuals to fill key positions in the future.

☐ Help the organization realign talent to meet its critical business needs.

☐ Ensure that the supply of talent equals the organization's demand.

☐ Help implement career development and talent management strategies to retain the organization's high-potential and high-performing employees.

☐ Help leaders diagnose development needs, identify training and development opportunities, and create a learning culture.

☐ Promote an environment where employees feel they make a difference, are valued, and are continuing to learn.

☐ Maximize efforts to retain the best people who can create, innovate, and move the organization forward.

For example, Pfizer worked with its district managers to spot people at risk for turnover and engage them in conversations about opportunities within the organization. After one year, a 2 percent drop in turnover saved the company $2.4 million in its training budget and brought a return of $3.6 million in cost avoidance and increased productivity (Galvin, Johnson, and Barbian, 2003).

Peter Senge, noted author and founding chair of the Society for Organizational Learning, says that everyone faces intense competition for key people:

Consider the predicament that some organizations find themselves in. Take, for example, the oil business. Who really wants to be in the business of drilling for oil and producing a product that inevitably produces global warming? What would make that something you'd want to do if you were a capable, young professional with a desire to make a positive contribution in the world? Perhaps, if you could be part of creating the next energy infrastructure, you might consider that part of your life's work.

So, forward-thinking companies will increasingly start to position themselves to be attractive to the best people that they want to draw in—people who truly want to contribute to economic, social, and environmental well-being.

How to Prepare

You are probably asking yourself, "So, what do I do now to better prepare myself for what's coming?" Figure 1-1 shows the seven factors that survey respondents believe will be most important for the WLP profession in the next three years. It paints a picture of what to expect in the near future and how the profession will be affected.

What's Next

Chapter 2 provides an overview of the ASTD Competency Model, which includes the competencies, areas of expertise, and roles that WLP practitioners will collectively play to succeed in the future.

Figure 1-1. Factors anticipated as important for the WLP profession, 2004–2006.

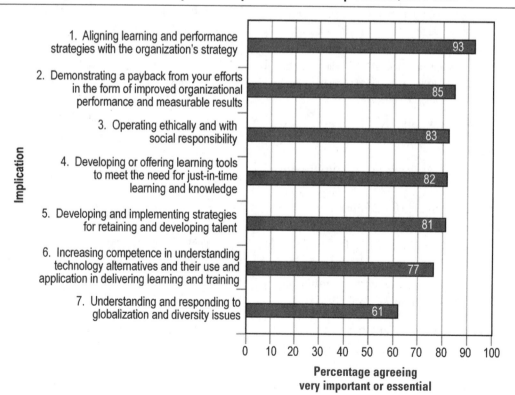

A Model for Today and the Future

The aim of many WLP professionals is to improve human performance. However, there are many different camps and philosophies regarding how human performance can and should be improved. For example, WLP professionals might choose to concentrate their efforts on individuals, groups, or the organization as a whole. Depending on their learning objective, the unit of analysis for change might command a broad or a narrow scope. Indeed, WLP professionals who choose to identify opportunities for improving performance might rely on very different tools, such as assessment, training, or coaching.

Any model of this dynamic and complex profession must capture the current reality but also point toward the future; things are simply moving too fast to do otherwise. Such a model must also encompass the sometimes conflicting perspectives of the pragmatic performance champions and those with their eyes on the long-term benefit for humankind. Given these challenges, it is important to maintain flexibility in defining the WLP profession. While the basic competencies required for effectiveness at the individual level may remain relatively stable, new paradigms and approaches will evolve and require integration into the model. The competency model presented in this report incorporates the current reality, identifies trends for the near future, and maintains flexibility for further enhancement as the profession continues to evolve.

This report paints a picture of what to expect over the next few years. It is an image that begs the need for a new competency model—a model that spells success for learning and performance practitioners now and in the years to come. Because the profession spans a range of expert areas of focus, the model (see figure 2-1) is broad enough to cover all WLP jobs, but it is not so broad that it can be applied to jobs outside the profession. It is also specific enough to outline real job requirements without making it irrelevant to some jobs in the WLP family. The model includes three layers of knowledge and skill areas: competencies, specific areas of professional expertise, and roles.

- **Competencies**—Clusters of skills, knowledge, abilities, and behaviors required for success across *all* WLP jobs. Competencies anchor the model because they are foundational in nature. Job success will be difficult to achieve without some level of expertise in the majority of these fundamental WLP competencies. Each competency in the model includes a definition and a list of key actions important for success.

- **Areas of expertise (AOEs)**—Specific technical and professional skills or knowledge required for success in WLP specialty areas. Although some WLP professionals are highly specialized, most demonstrate expertise in more than one AOE. AOEs are positioned above the competencies

Figure 2-1. ASTD Competency Model.

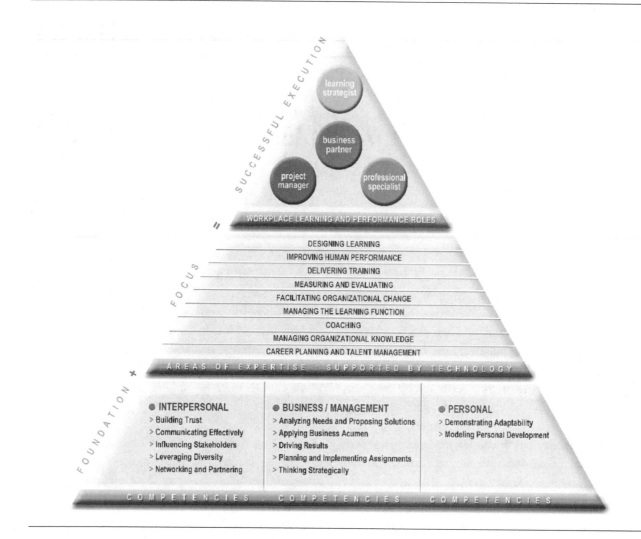

because they direct and supplement the foundational competencies through specialized skills and knowledge areas. All the AOEs rely on specialized technologies to leverage and support them. Each AOE in the model includes a definition, a list of key actions, and a list of key knowledge areas.

- **Roles**—Roles are broad areas of responsibility within the WLP profession that require a certain combination of competencies and AOEs to perform effectively. They are described in sensible, intuitive, and everyday language. Like competencies, roles can be demonstrated in the context of most WLP jobs. Roles are not the same as job titles; they are much more fluid, depending on the application or the project. For the WLP professional, playing the roles is analogous to maintaining a collection of hats—when the situation calls for it, the professional slips out of one role and "puts on" another.

For a full listing of the definitions, key actions, and key knowledge areas, see appendix A; for a full listing of every component in the model and its associated importance ratings, see appendix D.

Back to Basics

The ASTD Competency Model is built on several basic premises:

- *Applicable across organizational levels.* The model makes no distinctions regarding level or position. WLP professionals from the highest to the lowest organizational levels will find the content relevant to their jobs. The model does not list specific management skills, such as delegation or performance planning, because they are applicable to all professions in a generic sense and are not required skills of all WLP professionals. Those in management positions will need to supplement this model with competencies related to effective leadership and management skills.

- *The whole is greater than the sum of the parts.* The blend of competencies, AOEs, and roles adds power and utility to the model, just as the unique blend of competencies, AOEs, and roles defines the WLP profession and its boundaries. One could make the case that some competencies in the model are important for individuals in other professions. However, no other profession can claim this particular configuration of key actions, knowledge areas, and professional/technical skills.

- *A solid foundation.* As the data will show later in this report, the model is strongly supported and validated by thousands of WLP professionals. Practitioners can feel confident using it as a guide for managing their professional careers—from hiring to career development. Because it's impossible to craft a one-size-fits-all model, the need for some customization must be considered. However, the degree of customization needed should be minimal, because the model covers the large majority of relevant skills and knowledge for most WLP professionals. In fact, the more than 2,000 survey respondents indicated that, on average, the model covers 87 percent of the skills necessary for success in their current jobs.

- *The value of detail.* Each competency and AOE includes a carefully worded definition and a list of specific key actions. For the AOEs, key knowledge areas and lists of common outputs supplement the key actions. This level of specificity is an enhancement over previous studies in which competencies were presented only with general definitions. By clearly spelling out how the competencies, AOEs, and roles might be observed or demonstrated on the job, we gain a much clearer understanding of what WLP professionals actually do. Providing detail enables both measurement and development of competencies and encourages their application. Depending on the situation (for example, developing a curriculum), some WLP practitioners might need additional detail. If so, it would be necessary to delve a bit deeper, beyond the information provided in this report.

- *Back to the future.* Many argue that the WLP profession needs to transform itself to ensure long-term success. This model was designed with the future in mind—to convey what will be required for the next generation of practitioners to provide their organizations with an even higher level of value. While traditional conceptualizations of WLP jobs (for example, classroom trainers) are still relevant and important, there is room for evolving skills, knowledge, and new organizational roles (such as knowledge managers or performance consultants). By blending the profession's historical roots with evolving areas of growth, the model challenges thinking and promotes reexamination of current WLP jobs.

Hypothetically Speaking . . .

Let's drill down through a hypothetical organizational hierarchy—starting at the executive level—and look at a few examples of how the roles, AOEs, and competencies depicted in figure 2-1 might come into play for a few specific positions.

Example: Chief Learning Officer (CLO)

The CLO might focus on the Learning Strategist and Business Partner roles and rely on others to carry out the Project Manager and Professional Specialist roles. Because the CLO is likely to direct individuals in all AOEs, he or she probably needs some expertise in most—if not all nine—areas. In fact, the CLO might have had to gain experience and expertise in several AOEs before rising to the executive level. It would be logical to assume that the CLO has strong skills and knowledge in all the foundational competencies, and he or she might be especially strong in Thinking Strategically and Applying Business Acumen.

Example: External Consultant

Typically, organizations bring in consultants when they require additional expertise or resources. Although they are capable of playing many roles, external consultants might play one role exclusively. Depending on the assignment, a consultant could move freely from one role to another. Consultants sometimes play the Business Partner role to help others solidify a vision or strategy and to work internally with different groups.

Or, a consultant might move to the role of Professional Specialist when delivering a solution that is driven by a business strategy. All the foundational competencies are important for consultants, but they could require a high level of expertise in competencies such as Networking and Partnering and Analyzing Needs and Proposing Solutions.

Example: Corporate Trainer

Many people in this position spend the majority of their time in the Professional Specialist role. Some trainers might never play the role of Learning Strategist or Business Partner, but others—depending on their position—might do so occasionally. Because their AOE focus is Delivering Training, they might not have expertise in the other AOEs. Some foundational

Figure 2-2. Driving business performance.

competencies, such as Leveraging Diversity, Building Trust, and Communicating Effectively, are probably more important than others.

Reinventing the "Wheel"

Past ASTD competency studies have used a "wheel" graphic to represent how WLP fits into the larger picture of human resource management and other areas of organizational operations. Figure 2-2 depicts an updated version of that wheel.

The purpose of the wheel is to

- show what disciplines typically might be considered part of the WLP profession
- help define the WLP profession in relation to traditional HR disciplines.

At the hub is business strategy. Because all the traditional HR and organizational disciplines and AOEs making up the "spokes" contribute to an organization's success, they must be aligned with the business strategy. This alignment drives and contributes to business performance.

The left side of the wheel shows the AOEs, which represent the WLP professional disciplines. The bottom left portion highlights AOEs that focus primarily on learning and development solutions as the means to improving performance. Meanwhile, the upper left portion represents AOEs that are broader in focus and that might include solutions other than learning and development interventions. For example, a WLP professional who is facilitating organizational change might be operating in the context of an organization's need to restructure and change certain jobs. A professional who is expert in improving human performance might choose compensation and rewards and recognition as the primary solutions for improving performance.

Traditional HR disciplines appear in the upper right section of the wheel. Some of these include compensation and benefits as well as selection, staffing, and job design. The bottom right portion includes examples of other non-WLP or HR-related organizational functions such as sales, marketing, and customer services.

All organizational disciplines help drive business performance. As the WLP profession continues to evolve, practitioners will more likely begin to incorporate solutions from other organizational disciplines to help them maximize their contributions.

What's Next

This chapter provided an overview of the ASTD Competency Model. The next chapter is the first of three in-depth descriptions of each model component. Chapter 3 contains a detailed discussion of the model's bedrock component: the foundational competencies.

Chapter 3

Competencies

It all starts with the building blocks—competencies.

Competencies are the clusters of skills, knowledge, abilities, and behaviors required for job success. Workplace learning and performance professionals often use job competency models to guide their employee-development efforts. Similarly, competencies have many applications for organizations and individuals in the WLP profession. Organizations can use competencies to define selection criteria for new hires or placements in WLP positions and to guide their performance and development. Practitioners can use competencies as a roadmap to their own success on the job.

The study results have identified 12 competencies as essential for the majority of individuals in the WLP profession. As shown in this section of the ASTD Competency Model (figure 3-1), the foundational competencies are organized into three primary clusters: Interpersonal, Business/Management, and Personal.[1] The competencies are listed in alphabetical order within each cluster. Each competency also contains a list of key actions. In contrast, the key actions are presented in order of importance (see appendix A).

Defining the Relevant Behaviors

Foundational competencies define the relevant behaviors for *all* WLP professionals. To varying degrees, everyone in the profession must display some aspect of each competency. For example, it is difficult to imagine any WLP professional being successful without the ability to build trust or be adaptable. However, how these competencies are used can depend on the particular job held by the professional.

The following illustrations show how the foundational competency Applying Business Acumen has relevance

Figure 3-1. Foundational competencies.

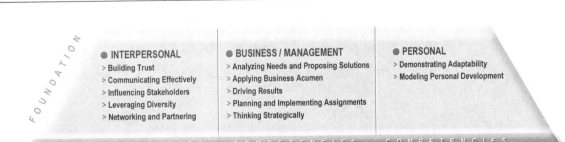

for both a chief learning officer and an instructional designer.

- *Chief learning officer*—As executives, CLOs are often charged with helping to make strategic decisions regarding business operations. They must apply business acumen to decide what learning system will need to be in place to meet future business goals or to decide whether a particular learning function should be handled in-house or outsourced. Often, the CLO sits on the organization's operating committee to help guide all strategic talent decisions.
- *Instructional designer*—Designers should be aware of factors affecting the business, because those issues might have a bearing on the type of learning content that is appropriate. Instructional designers often need to think of meaningful examples that provide context for the learning experience. An understanding of operations helps

them link learning content to on-the-job activities. Although instructional designers might have less need for applying financial data, they would still value that information for certain situations. Some instructional designers must justify spending and development costs; others need to incorporate financial principles into learning content.

Although the competencies in the ASTD Competency Model are foundational, few professionals will be strong in every one. Because all WLP professionals—regardless of level or experience—have unique strengths and development needs relative to the overall competency profile, it's impossible to construct a model that applies perfectly to everyone. Instead, the model is designed to cover most of the relevant skills and knowledge areas for a large majority of people in the profession. As mentioned earlier, on average, respondents indicated that the model covers 87 percent of the skills necessary for success in their current jobs.

Figure 3-2. Current importance of WLP competencies.

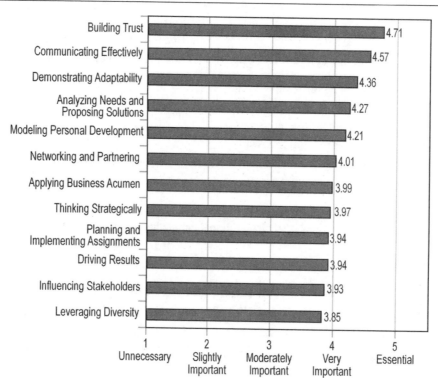

What's Important?

In a ranking of overall importance, competencies from the Interpersonal and Personal categories appear at the top of the list: Building Trust, Communicating Effectively, and Demonstrating Adaptability. Survey respondents rated each competency in terms of its importance for effectiveness in their current job. Figure 3-2 shows the average current importance rating for all 12 competencies. All the competencies are more than moderately important (that is, rated 3.0 or above), and no one competency is dramatically more important than the others. The ranking of the competencies is relatively stable and shows very few differences in importance across organizational level (for example, executive, individual contributor), specialty area (for example, training, coaching), and industry (for example, manufacturing, consulting). Additional analyses show that the importance of competencies is not affected by age, race, gender, or national origin (see appendix D).

Looking to the Future

While the model for success has evolved significantly in the past few years, WLP professionals foresee even greater change looming in the next three years. When asked which competencies will become most important in the future, WLP professionals identified the following (see figure 3-3 and appendix D):

1. Analyzing Needs and Proposing Solutions
2. Thinking Strategically
3. Communicating Effectively
4. Driving Results.

These findings represent a marked departure from the competencies deemed most important for today. Two of the top competencies for the future, Thinking Strategically and Driving Results, are ranked eighth and 10th in terms of importance for today's jobs—a considerable jump up the ladder! This means that WLP professionals foresee the need to do a better job

Figure 3-3. Future importance of WLP competencies.

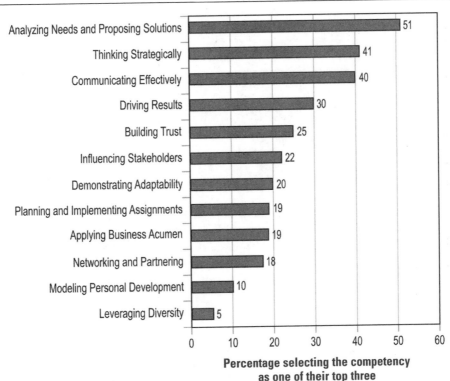

Percentage selecting the competency
as one of their top three

of monitoring internal and external influences on learning and performance, tracking new industry trends, and considering systems issues (Thinking Strategically). They also need to hone their ability to identify opportunities for improvement, set well-defined goals related to learning and performance solutions, and monitor their progress (Driving Results).

What's Next

Chapter 4 contains a detailed discussion of the AOEs—the specific technical and professional skills and knowledge required for success in WLP specialty areas.

---

[1] The three clusters used in the model were formed based on a combination of conceptual and statistical analyses. In the ASTD Competency Model, statistical factor analyses show that the 12 competencies cluster into two primary groupings: Business/Management and Interpersonal. Although the competencies identified as Personal and Interpersonal tended to cluster together, the two personal competencies were separated to illustrate that they are more likely to be driven by personality traits and, therefore, might be more difficult to develop.

Chapter 4

Areas of Expertise

The middle section of the ASTD Competency Model (see figure 4-1) includes areas of expertise, which are defined as the specific technical and professional skills and knowledge required for success in WLP specialty areas. Think of AOEs as the knowledge and skills an individual must have above and beyond the foundational competencies. To function effectively in a given AOE, a person must display a blend of the appropriate foundational competencies and unique technical/professional skills and knowledge. The model lists the AOEs in order of descending importance for current job effectiveness as perceived by respondents to the validation survey.

It's About Time

In the model, the AOEs reflect the natural evolution of the WLP profession. As organizations evolve, new technologies emerge, and individual needs change, WLP professionals often are asked to take on new responsibilities and readjust their focus. Some specialty areas remain fairly stable over time, while others change significantly. For example, over the past decade the skills required to measure performance improvement have become more important. The AOEs presented in this report reflect how WLP professionals currently focus their work and also describe practices that are becoming increasingly important.

It's All Relative to the Job

Although all nine AOEs are important (that is, having an average importance rating of 3.0 or higher; see figure 4-2), it is unlikely that all would be equally important for all jobs. Effective performance of one's job might not require any expertise in certain areas.

Some AOEs might draw a lower importance rating by WLP professionals as a group because they are not used

Figure 4-1. Areas of expertise.

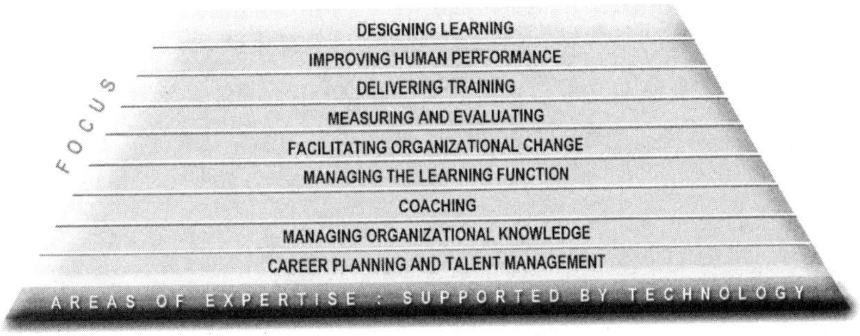

DESIGNING LEARNING
IMPROVING HUMAN PERFORMANCE
DELIVERING TRAINING
MEASURING AND EVALUATING
FACILITATING ORGANIZATIONAL CHANGE
MANAGING THE LEARNING FUNCTION
COACHING
MANAGING ORGANIZATIONAL KNOWLEDGE
CAREER PLANNING AND TALENT MANAGEMENT

FOCUS

AREAS OF EXPERTISE: SUPPORTED BY TECHNOLOGY

as frequently. In fact, WLP professionals are much more likely to provide higher importance ratings for AOEs in which they spend more time. However, it is important to note that *time spent* and *importance* are not synonymous. It is possible to spend very little time in areas that are essential to effective job performance and vice versa. The key point to remember is that although perceived importance and time spent are both relative to the individual's job, *all* the AOEs in this report are important and relevant for the profession.

Almost all (95 percent) of WLP professionals' work responsibilities can be classified into one or more of the nine AOEs. Figure 4-3 shows the average percentage of time respondents spend in each AOE. (Survey respondents were asked to allocate 100 points to indicate the percentage of time they spend in each of the AOEs or in other activities.) It is not surprising that, on average, most WLP professionals spend the largest share of their time in the Designing Learning and Delivering Training AOEs. After all, the profession

was born with a training focus, and it remains a mainstay. Almost half of the survey respondents identified either Designing Learning or Delivering Training as their primary AOE. While the popularity of these AOEs is readily evident, it's also clear that many WLP professionals spend their time in more than one AOE. In fact, 63 percent of professionals spend at least 10 percent of their time in three to five AOEs. This indicates that WLP practitioners are often providing expertise in multiple areas and must apply a broad range of skills. This is a key insight. Success in the profession is no longer defined by solid delivery or instructional design skills; workplace learning and performance is truly becoming a more complex and multidisciplinary profession.

Each AOE represents a distinct area of practice with unique outputs and knowledge areas, and each assumes the use of certain methods and operating processes. Unlike with competencies, an individual does not have to be expert in every AOE to be considered successful.

Figure 4-2. Importance of AOEs.

Figure 4-3. Percentage of time spent in each AOE.

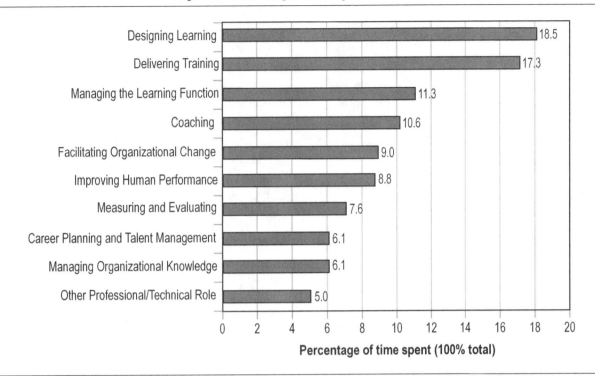

However, most professionals will demonstrate a high level of expertise in more than one AOE and would benefit from a strong working knowledge of all the AOEs.

Supported by Technology

The emergence of new technology has exerted a powerful influence on the evolution of the WLP profession. Technology has become a critical skill and knowledge area. Enabling technology—such as Web-based programs that deliver synchronous and asynchronous learning, wireless access, automated evaluations, online coaching, and use of a learning management system (LMS) to track learning content—has dramatically altered how WLP professionals work.

Some professionals might even consider technology to be an AOE. However, in developing the model, it quickly became clear that technology is not separate from the AOEs. Instead, it is an enabler that opens additional avenues for delivering WLP solutions. Technology without context has little value; only

through the expression of technology in WLP applications is its real power seen. The fundamental assumption is that all WLP professionals need to keep abreast of the latest technology trends; thus, the selection and use of appropriate technologies is embedded into the AOE key knowledge areas and key actions. In this way technological competence is positioned as a valuable asset for all WLP professionals as they strive for efficient execution of their AOEs. Indeed, such expertise will only become more important in the future.

Keys to Unlock the AOEs

Each AOE includes a list of key knowledge areas and key actions (see appendix A), presented in descending order of importance. Key knowledge areas list the range of theoretical and procedural knowledge required for success in the AOE. Because there is so much depth of knowledge for each AOE, the ASTD Competency Model does not list specific theories or approaches unless they are particularly important for the AOE.

Key actions list the behaviors and activities required for an individual to function effectively in the AOE. Usually, key actions are readily observable and portray the daily work of WLP professionals in each AOE. Experts in each specialty area have validated all the key knowledge areas and actions. A review of the ratings shows that the AOEs have a high degree of validity (see appendix D). All AOEs received an average rating of at least "Moderately Important" (3.0). (See figure 4-2.)

What Does the Future Hold?

Because the workplace learning and performance profession has deep roots in the training field, some practitioners immediately think of learning solutions when addressing human performance issues. Today, however, many WLP professionals are expanding their scope to include solutions beyond the domain of traditional learning interventions.

This trend is readily apparent when examining the AOEs that are likely to become more important in the next three years (see figure 4-4). Survey respondents were asked to select the one AOE that would become more important for effective performance of their jobs in the next three years. The top-rated AOEs (Improving Human Performance and Facilitating Organizational Change) do not always employ learning as a primary solution. Because these top two are outside what is traditionally viewed as core "learning" AOEs, it stands to reason that the "L" and the "P" in WLP are meant to be complementary, and that the future of the profession points to a greater synergy between learning and performance.

Projected changes for the future confirm the evolution of the WLP profession and how it is defined. The profession originated as training with an emphasis on equipping employees with the knowledge and skills they needed to do their work. Over time, the term

Figure 4-4. Most important AOEs for the future (2004-2006).

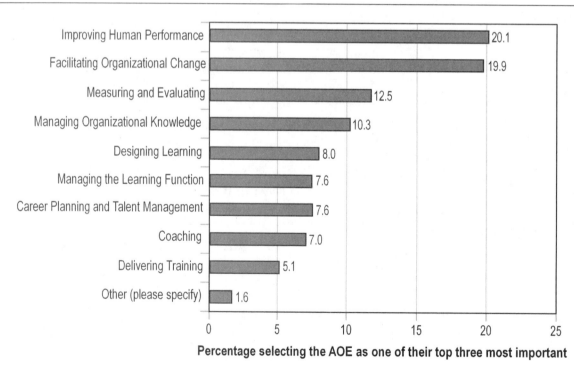

Percentage selecting the AOE as one of their top three most important

workplace learning and performance has replaced and subsumed *human resource development* and *training and development*. By linking two terms together in a single phrase—*learning and performance*—the name of the profession reflects a balance between activity-focused interventions, such as training, and a results-oriented focus on learning as a means to achieving improved business results. More than ever before, organizations now expect WLP professionals to understand the business and align learning, development, performance-improvement strategies, and evaluation with overall business strategies in order to contribute to enhanced business results.

What's Next

Chapter 5 explains the four roles—Learning Strategist, Business Partner, Project Manager, and Professional Specialist—and how they fit into the ASTD Competency Model. It also illustrates how the roles link to competencies.

Chapter 5

Four Roles

This report defines roles as broad areas of responsibility within the WLP profession that require a certain combination of competencies and AOEs to perform effectively. For example, someone playing the Learning Strategist role must draw on several competencies and AOEs to be successful. Like competencies, roles can be demonstrated in the context of most WLP jobs. Roles are not the same as job titles; they are much more fluid, depending on the application or the project. Roles are described in sensible, intuitive, and everyday language. While competencies provide details around specific key actions, roles reflect how those competencies are applied to meet responsibilities within the work environment.

The study identified four roles for the ASTD Competency Model (see figure 5-1):

- **Learning Strategist**—Determines how workplace learning and performance improvement can best be leveraged to achieve long-term business success and add value to meet organizational needs; leads in the planning and implementation of learning and performance improvement strategies that support the organization's strategic direction and that are based on an analysis of the effectiveness of existing learning and performance-improvement strategies.
- **Business Partner**—Applies business and industry knowledge to partner with the client in iden-

tifying workplace performance-improvement opportunities; evaluates possible solutions and recommends solutions that will have a positive impact on performance; gains client agreement and commitment to the proposed solutions and collaboratively develops an overall implementation strategy that includes evaluating impact on business performance; uses appropriate interpersonal styles and communication methods to build effective long-term relationships with the client.
- **Project Manager**—Plans, resources, and monitors the effective delivery of learning and performance solutions in a way that supports the overall business venture; communicates purpose, ensures effective execution of an implementation plan, removes barriers, ensures adequate support, and follows up.
- **Professional Specialist**—Designs, develops, delivers, or evaluates learning and performance solutions; maintains and applies an in-depth working knowledge in any one or more of the workplace learning and performance specialty AOEs—Career Planning and Talent Management, Coaching, Delivering Training, Designing Learning, Facilitating Organizational Change, Improving Human Performance, Managing Organizational Knowledge, Managing the Learning Function, and Measuring and Evaluating.

Figure 5-1. Four WLP roles.

The four roles illustrate both the strategic (Learning Strategist and Business Partner) and the operational (Project Manager and Professional Specialist) sides of the profession. These roles are applicable to positions across the profession, from consultant to educator. Compared with past ASTD studies, these roles reflect efforts to simplify the model and strengthen the emphasis on business performance and business partnering. To achieve strong business performance, WLP professionals—acting as business partners—must align business goals with the design and implementation of learning strategy goals. By being solid business partners, WLP professionals make sure that the right solutions for the business are identified and implemented.

Playing by the Roles

As mentioned earlier, roles are not unique to one person in an organization, and WLP professionals might play multiple roles, depending on the situation. (Recall the hat analogy from chapter 2.) In fact, more than 90 percent of survey respondents indicate that they play each role at least some of the time. Figure 5-2 confirms that most professionals spend an almost equal amount of time in each role.

As might be expected, the importance of the roles for effectiveness in one's current job varies depending on the organizational level/function. Table 5-1 illustrates that professionals at more senior levels are the most likely to spend time in the Learning Strategist and Business Partner roles. Managers, supervisors, and team leaders tend to focus on the Project Manager role, and individual contributors see the greatest importance in the Professional Specialist role. Independent consultants are more likely to work as Business Partners and Professional Specialists. These ratings of importance relative to level/function make sense and add to the validity of the roles. It is important to remember, however, that the roles are not unique to any one level or position, and all have consistently high importance ratings.

Most WLP professionals spend the largest share of their time (28 percent) in the Professional Specialist role (see figure 5-2). More than half (53 percent) spend at least 25 percent of their time in this role. It's also the role with the highest overall importance rating (see table 5-1). The Professional Specialist role was created to acknowledge that WLP professionals spend much of their time designing, developing, and delivering workplace learning and performance solutions. Strategy and partnering are important, but almost all jobs have a strong focus on implementation.

Validating the Roles

In the current model, survey respondents indicate that the roles cover about 93 percent of WLP job responsibilities. All roles have importance ratings far above the minimum average score of 3.5 (ratings were made on a 5-point scale, with 1 being "unnecessary" and 5 being "essential"). Additionally, WLP professionals spend a

Figure 5-2. Percentage of time WLP professionals spend in each role.

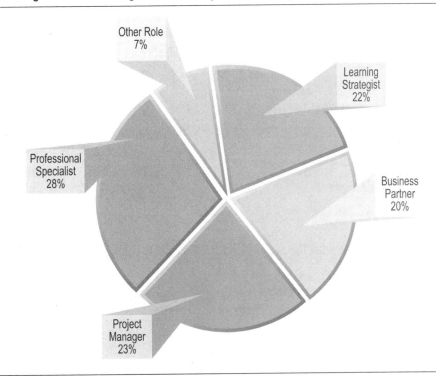

significant amount of their time (at least 20 percent) in all four roles. Importance ratings of the roles reveal very few differences across specialty areas (for example, training, coaching) or industries (for example, manufacturing, consulting). Additional analyses show that the importance of roles is not affected by rater age, race, gender, or national origin (see appendix D).

Linking Roles and Competencies

As defined previously, roles are broad areas of responsibility that require a certain combination of compe-

tencies and AOEs to perform effectively. Thus, it is important to understand which competencies are most important for particular roles. Most competencies have some relevance for each role. For example, it is easy to see that a competency such as Communicating Effectively is important to the successful execution of all four roles. However, some roles rely more on certain competencies than others.

Table 5-2 presents the correlations between importance ratings of roles and competencies from the survey data. The numbers in the table are correlation coefficients

Table 5-1. Importance of role by organizational level/function.

Role	Overall	Executives & Directors	Managers	Supervisors & Team Leaders	Individual Contributors	Independent Consultants
Learning Strategist	4.01	4.22	4.13	3.97	3.83	4.14
Business Partner	3.98	4.31	3.96	3.86	3.86	4.38
Project Manager	4.08	4.19	4.21	4.25	3.96	4.05
Professional Specialist	4.19	4.11	4.17	4.36	4.25	4.39

Note: All ratings were made on a 5-point scale (1 = Unnecessary, 5 = Essential).

with a possible range of −1.0 to 1.0. The closer the correlation coefficient is to 1.0, the stronger the positive relationship between the competency and the role. The table highlights the strongest correlations between each competency and role. In each row, the role with the strongest relationship to a competency is highlighted in darker gray. The second strongest correlation is highlighted in lighter gray. For example, the competency Driving Results most strongly correlates with the Learning Strategist role (darker gray), followed by Business Partner (lighter gray). This means that competence in Driving Results is a critical component for successful execution of the Learning Strategist role.

When examining the pattern of correlations, we see that each role requires a unique combination, or mosaic, of competencies. The Learning Strategist and Business Partner roles have the strongest relationship to the Business/Management competencies. Additionally, the Business Partner role includes a relatively stronger focus on the Interpersonal cluster of competencies. One of the main responsibilities of someone in the Business Partner role is to work with key stakeholders to ensure the

Table 5-2. Correlation between roles and competencies.

	Learning Strategist	Business Partner	Project Manager	Professional Specialist	High/Low Difference
Business/Management					
Analyzing Needs and Proposing Solutions	0.36	0.40	0.31	0.22	0.18
Applying Business Acumen	0.31	0.40	0.23	0.05	0.34
Driving Results	0.34	0.31	0.27	0.14	0.21
Planning and Implementing Assignments	0.20	0.19	0.39	0.18	0.21
Thinking Strategically	0.40	0.33	0.21	0.14	0.26
Interpersonal					
Building Trust	0.17	0.19	0.16	0.15	0.04
Communicating Effectively	0.13	0.12	0.15	0.22	0.10
Influencing Stakeholders	0.31	0.37	0.27	0.12	0.25
Leveraging Diversity	0.16	0.13	0.14	0.16	0.03
Networking and Partnering	0.20	0.25	0.21	0.16	0.10
Personal					
Demonstrating Adaptability	0.19	0.17	0.16	0.20	0.04
Modeling Personal Development	0.18	0.07	0.11	0.22	0.15

Note: In each row, the role highlighted in darker gray has the strongest relationship to the competency. The role highlighted in lighter gray has the second strongest relationship.

Sample sizes used to compute the correlations range from 1,481 to 1,670. All correlations in the table are statistically significant.

success of solutions. As one would expect, the Project Manager role has the strongest relationship to the Planning and Implementing Assignments competency. Finally, the Professional Specialist role shows the strongest relationships to the Personal competencies and several of the Interpersonal competencies. Professional Specialists often work one-on-one with individuals or groups, thus requiring strong communication skills.

In table 5-2, the column labeled "High/Low Difference" shows the difference between the strongest and weakest correlations. Larger values indicate that there is greater variance in the relationship between particular competencies and roles. Values approaching zero indicate that the competency has a fairly consistent relationship across all the roles. Some competencies are universally important across all roles. These broadly applicable competencies include Leveraging Diversity, Demonstrating Adaptability, and Building Trust. In other words, effective performance of these competencies is important for everyone in every role.

The competencies with the greatest high/low difference are less universally important. These competencies include Applying Business Acumen, Thinking Strategically, and Influencing Stakeholders. Depending on the role, these three competencies might have a strong or a weak relationship to successful execution of the role. For example, Applying Business Acumen does not have a very strong relationship to success in the Professional Specialist role (correlation of 0.05). However, it is very important in the Business Partner role (correlation of 0.40).

What's Next

Chapter 6 describes how WLP leaders, educators, and individual contributors can leverage the ASTD Competency Model to optimize their recruitment, succession planning, selection, performance management, and career development efforts.

Chapter 6

Realizing the Value

The competencies, AOEs, and roles defined in this report pinpoint the behaviors, knowledge, and responsibilities that are critical for workplace learning and performance professionals. The real value of the WLP competencies and AOEs is realized in their application. WLP professionals need to work within their organizations to incorporate the roles, competencies, and AOEs into their own human resource systems to

- attract people into the profession
- evaluate individuals for selection or promotion
- diagnose training and development needs
- design training and development programs
- guide career-planning decisions
- guide coaching and feedback
- assess job performance
- establish a foundation for credentialing programs.

The competencies and AOEs in this study serve as a common framework on which WLP human resource systems can be integrated and become more focused, efficient, and flexible. For example, a WLP hiring manager can use the appropriate competencies and AOEs to select a new employee who is able to demonstrate the desired competencies and professional expertise. Once the individual is hired, the same list of competencies and AOEs can be used in the performance management system to monitor and evaluate performance on the job. Competencies that are rated as needing improvement can serve as the basis for choosing appropriate training and development activities.

And once WLP professionals know the competencies and AOEs needed for successful performance, they can become more self-directed in their development.

More than 30 years ago, Bill Byham, founder and CEO of DDI, began advocating the use of competencies as the foundation for taking a systems approach to human resource activities. Figure 6-1 depicts the HR systems that can be built around competencies and AOEs. Various human resource systems can be crafted into one integrated system by relating each to a common set of competencies and AOEs. The graphic shows the competencies and AOEs at the core or hub, surrounded by some of the major HR systems that can be built around them. Because the same competency/AOE model underpins all parts of the system, each part operates more efficiently, training costs decrease, and managers—because they are speaking a common "competency language"—learn each new element more quickly. As an added benefit, the image of the entire system as well as HR is enhanced.

How to Use the Model with Clients

The ASTD Competency Model provides business leaders and clients (both external and internal) at all levels with an in-depth profile for success for effective WLP professionals. The model serves as a valuable educational tool for clients. By thoroughly reviewing the competencies, clients can understand how their WLP partners are expected to think strategically and help drive business results. Thus, clients can readily see

Figure 6-1. HR systems that can be built around competencies and AOEs.

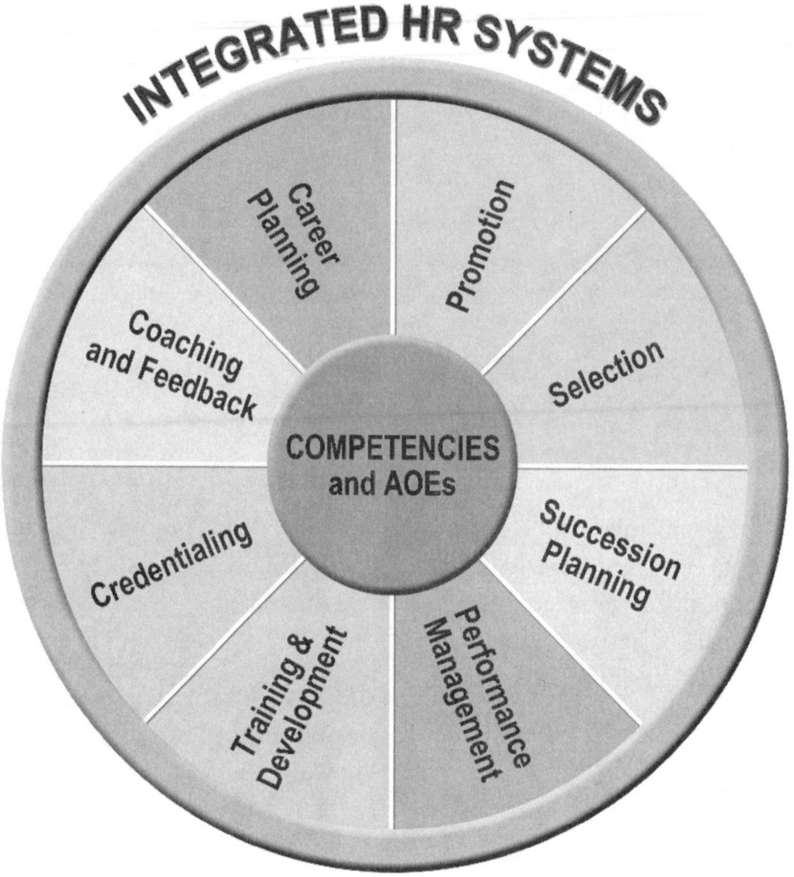

the potential value of a partnership. Once clients understand the WLP Business/Management competencies (Analyzing Needs and Proposing Solutions, Applying Business Acumen, Driving Results, Planning and Implementing Assignments, and Thinking Strategically), they can hold their WLP partners accountable for demonstrating these behaviors.

Clients are in a unique position to raise the performance bar of the WLP profession by demanding that its practitioners understand their business, recognize their business priorities, target appropriate improvement opportunities, and make a positive impact on their business results. This understanding will enhance the image of the profession as a legitimate discipline that adds value.

The ASTD Competency Model also can help clients better understand what's expected of them when identifying and implementing performance-improvement strategies within their own businesses. For example, by reviewing the definition and key actions for the Facilitating Organizational Change AOE (see appendix A), the business manager/client will grasp the importance of clearly defining the desired outcomes from the improvement strategy, having a contract for change with their WLP partner, serving as a sponsor and spokesperson for the intervention or program, and actively supporting the change effort. This heightened understanding will increase the client's level of involvement in the implementation and will improve its business impact. Ultimately, true partnering will occur and lead to better bottom-line results.

How WLP Leaders Can Use the Model

For CLOs or other WLP managers, the ASTD Competency Model can serve as a template for success today and in the future. The model may be used to determine which competencies and AOEs are appropriate for a unit's WLP professionals. Leaders may also use it to assess the extent to which their professionals are demonstrating the competencies and effectively performing in the relevant AOEs. A comparison of existing talent against the model will identify individuals' strengths and development needs and those of their particular team.

Managers in the profession must demand excellence from their staff—whether they are internal resources or external vendors and partners. (The model applies to both.) This means that leaders ultimately must challenge all WLP professionals to effectively demonstrate all 12 foundational competencies and any AOEs within their responsibility. Chances are that such a profile of proficiency is not the current state of affairs and that development, assessment, and coaching will be required of leaders to help their staffs achieve that level of excellence.

WLP leaders are responsible for ensuring that practitioners are competent and held in demand by business leaders. One way to do this is to encourage professionals to expand and enhance their skills. The ASTD Competency Model is more future oriented and strategic than previous competency models; to embrace the future, managers need to integrate the competencies and AOEs into their human resource systems. Doing so raises performance expectations and provides a common link throughout the organization's human resource systems. Integrating the competencies and AOEs provides a powerful means of ensuring that all systems promote and reinforce the same set of knowledge, skills, and abilities that are important for achieving business results.

Selection and Promotion

For those in WLP management, hiring and promoting the most qualified professionals is key to future success. The cost of hiring the wrong person is significant. The rule of thumb is that the cost of a poor hire ranges from the individual's salary (for entry-level positions) to four times the salary (for senior-level positions). Successful selection and promotion decisions hinge on using the right selection criteria. As mentioned earlier, the competencies and AOEs defined in this study have been validated by more than 2,000 WLP professionals and are the right criteria for gathering complete behavioral information about candidates for selection or promotion. The first step is to review the competencies and AOEs relative to the position to determine which are important for success. Then, selection or promotion systems can be designed around them, provided additional validation work is done for customized systems.

Almost all organizations include interviews in their selection systems. These interviews should be structured to guide data gathering around the appropriate competencies and AOEs needed in the targeted position. Interview guides should provide a variety of questions for each targeted competency and AOE so that the interviewer can collect enough behavioral examples to evaluate how effectively the candidate has demonstrated the desired behaviors in similar past situations. After all, past behavior predicts future behavior. Of course, a good interview process also should include a review of the candidate's job samples (for example, training programs the person has designed or instructor evaluation forms).

Figure 6-2 shows an example of a competency-based interview guide for the competency Building Trust. The guide includes the competency definition and key actions as well as a list of several planned behavioral questions. The interviewer collects the behavioral examples from the applicant by using the appropriate column in the guide to document the situation or task, the applicant's action, and the ensuing result.

Additionally, behavioral simulations can be designed to give interviewers an opportunity to observe candidates performing in typical on-the-job situations. For example, a client-partnering simulation could be developed to enable an applicant to demonstrate various key actions related to competencies, such as Influencing Stakeholders, Communicating Effectively, and Building Trust. Someone who is being considered

Figure 6-2. Sample interview guide for the Building Trust competency.

Building Trust

Interacting with others in a way that gives them confidence in one's intentions and those of the organization.

Key Actions

— *Operates with integrity*
— *Discloses position*
— *Maintains confidentiality*
— *Leads by example*
— *Treats people fairly*
— *Ensures compliance with legal, ethical, and regulatory requirements*

Planned Behavioral Questions

1. There are many inequities that exist at work (e.g., workloads, compensation, expectations, etc.). Describe some of the inequities you've observed at work. What did you do?

2. Often there are people in an organization who deserve more credit than they receive. Tell me about a time when this happened. What did you do?

3. We don't always work with people who are ethical or honest. Give me an example of a time when you saw another employee do something that you thought was inappropriate. What did you do? What happened?

★ Situation/Task	Action	Result

Communication:

Building Trust Rating: _____

for a trainer's job could be required to participate in a training presentation simulation that would enable the applicant to demonstrate the Delivering Training AOE and competencies such as Demonstrating Adaptability and Leveraging Diversity.

To accurately evaluate performance related to specific competencies or AOEs, interviewers or assessors usually receive training. Evaluators need to be able to

- accurately and reliably classify observed behavior into the appropriate competency or AOE
- evaluate the quality of each behavioral example
- assign a rating for the competency or AOE based on all the data provided and the rating scale being used.

The level of evaluator expertise required for various human resource applications might vary, but an evaluator at least must be competent in each of the above areas.

Figure 6-3 illustrates what a competency- and AOE-based coverage grid might look like in the selection of a workplace learning and performance professional. The competencies and the Delivering Training AOE are listed on the left; the steps of the selection process appear at the top and run from start (phone screen) to finish (reference check). The Xs indicate the methods used to evaluate each competency and the AOE.

Evaluators should be trained to use such competency- and AOE-based selection tools effectively and to accurately and consistently evaluate the information gathered. Doing so greatly increases their likelihood of making good selection and promotion decisions. A well-designed selection or promotion system based on competencies and AOEs ensures that the right people are in the right jobs from the very start. This reduces turnover and has measurable bottom-line impact.

Training and Development

WLP leaders can use the list of competencies and AOEs to help create individual development plans for their direct reports. First, they would use the ASTD Competency Model to prioritize their direct reports'

development needs and to evaluate the applicability and quality of training and development programs. Then they would map training and development opportunities to their direct reports' top development needs. Like selection and promotion, training and development activities can be more effective when organized by competencies and AOEs. The list in this study allows the WLP manager to ask, "Do our programs address all the key actions of the competencies/AOEs required for success? Do they do so effectively?" Where gaps exist in the current training and development curricula, additional training can be developed or purchased.

The competency/AOE list also can be used to identify individual or group training and development needs. Matching the appropriate training and development intervention or program to an individual requires an assessment process that determines how the person measures up relative to the list. The assessment could be the WLP manager's thoughtful evaluation based on performance data and job observation, or it could be based on an assessment center or a multirater assessment tool (for example, 360°) designed to measure

Figure 6-3. Sample competency and AOE coverage grid for a WLP professional.

	Phone Screen	Manager Interview	Training Presentation Simulation	Client Partnering Simulation	CLO Interview	Reference Check
Influencing Stakeholders		X		X	X	X
Communicating Effectively	X	X	X	X	X	
Delivering Training		X	X			X
Planning & Implementing Assignments	X	X	X	X		
Applying Business Acumen		X		X	X	
Demonstrating Adaptability	X		X			
Building Trust		X	X	X	X	X
Networking & Partnering	X		X	X		X
Thinking Stragetically		X		X	X	X
Leveraging Diversity		X	X			X

the competency/AOE list. The same tools can be used before or after the intervention to determine its effectiveness.

Career and Succession Planning

The competencies and AOEs in the model also can play a valuable part in career and succession planning. To effectively use it as such, WLP managers first need to look at the jobs in their purview and determine which competencies and AOEs are required for each job. This information should be made accessible to current WLP practitioners as well as to other employees considering the profession. Also, tools should be made available to employees, who would assess themselves against the AOEs and competencies to gauge their proficiency against the job requirements. Based on how closely proficiency matches requirements, managers could encourage employees to apply for a particular position, help them define self-development goals, or identify appropriate "stretch" assignments to prepare them for the next job or future organizational needs.

When managers encourage career and succession planning, they are actively supporting talent growth and talent retention in the profession. They are preparing for the future—ensuring that they will have talent ready to move the people who are in more operational roles, such as the Professional Specialist role, into more strategic roles, such as Learning Strategist.

Performance Management

Competencies and AOEs can play an integral role in an organization's performance management system. Managers can include the appropriate competencies or AOEs in WLP professionals' performance plans, provide feedback on them throughout the year, and rate them in a year-end performance review. For this type of system to be effective, managers must make sure the performance management process is balanced; that is, each person's performance plan must include both objectives and competencies/AOEs.

A balanced performance management system ensures employee accountability, clarity, and focus in meeting individual goals, business objectives, and department goals. Employees need to have a clear understanding of

the behaviors that they are expected to display in their daily activities. They also need to know that *how* they behave (competencies/AOEs) is just as important as *what* they achieve (objectives). The competencies and AOEs in this report are defined with key actions that spell out performance expectations (see appendix A). The key actions delineate exactly how employees must behave to be effective. They also set the stage for the WLP leader to provide feedback and coaching, both of which contribute to an individual's ongoing development. For example, telling a trainer that she needs to improve average course evaluation ratings does not necessarily help her know what specifically to do differently. It's more helpful and meaningful for the manager to coach and provide feedback on key actions for the AOE Delivering Training. Such feedback might describe how the trainer could "encourage learner participation," "build learner motivation," and "establish her own credibility as an instructor."

WLP managers also must be sure that their direct reports or those in dotted-line reporting relationships understand what competencies/AOEs they need to develop to improve performance or prepare for a changing role. Once a manager and direct report agree on developmental competencies or AOEs, they should identify specific objectives and include them in the performance plan to ensure that appropriate development occurs. Figure 6-4 shows a sample development plan that reflects the AOEs and key actions on which a WLP professional wanted to focus his development efforts. For each AOE, two objectives were agreed upon and executed during the course of the performance cycle.

How Individual Contributors Can Use the Model

"Am I performing effectively today, and am I ready for the future?" is the question that every WLP individual contributor should be asking. One of the most direct ways to answer this question is to assess current performance against the WLP competencies. The ASTD Competency Model clearly describes what competencies professionals should have today and in the future.

Figure 6-4. Sample development plan for a WLP professional.

Development Plan

Competency/AOE: Designing Learning

Key Actions	Objectives	
• Analyzes and selects technologies • Integrates technology options	• Develop in-depth knowledge about how to design e-learning simulations by the end of second quarter.	☒ Completed
	• Incorporate an e-learning simulation in the design of the new sales training program before end of fourth quarter.	☒ Completed
More development in this competency needed? ☐ Yes ☒ No		

Competency/AOE: Facilitating Organizational Change

Key Actions	Objectives	
• Facilitates strategic planning for change • Builds involvement	• Organize and lead the process improvement task force and achieve its goal to identify and implement improvements in sales support systems by the end of the fiscal year.	☒ Completed
	• Work with the Sales VP to jointly create and implement a communication plan about the new sales support systems by end of second quarter.	☒ Completed
More development in this competency needed? ☐ Yes ☒ No		

© Development Dimensions Int'l, Inc., MCMXCIX.

Start With Self-Assessment

A good first step is to perform a self-assessment against the foundational competencies. This can be done by first reading the competency definition and key actions and then rating current performance on a simple 3-point scale (1 = needs development, 2 = demonstrates effective performance, and 3 = strength). For competencies rated as "needs development," the individual decides which two or three are most important and then meets with his or her manager to agree on appropriate developmental activities. The WLP professional and manager also discuss the competencies rated as strengths and agree on how best to leverage them for the most profound impact on department and business unit goals.

The CD: A Handy Reference

The nine AOEs cover all the WLP professional specialty areas. Because few WLP professionals are expert in all areas, there is always room to grow. It is a best practice for a WLP professional to identify an AOE for improvement and create an individual development plan with his or her manager. The CD-ROM provided with this book can help with that development effort. The CD includes the competency dictionary found in appendix A and serves as a convenient, digital source of reference information. Its contents include all the definitions, key actions, and key knowledge areas that a WLP professional would need when creating a development plan.

WLP professionals must position themselves to add quantifiable value to organizational performance. One of the best ways for individual contributors to enhance their value to the organization is to take responsibility for their own development. By continually learning and renewing their skills, they will achieve greater versatility, more job satisfaction, and, ultimately, career success and marketability. The ASTD Competency Model provides an excellent structure for managing current performance, identifying competency gaps, determining developmental needs, measuring progress, and preparing for the future.

How Educators Can Use the Model

Many organizations and learning institutions—including colleges, universities, business schools, professional associations, and consulting firms—are committed to advancing the workplace learning and performance profession by developing practitioners in the field. The competency and AOE definitions plus the key actions serve as an excellent tool for evaluating current curricula and planning new offerings. The ASTD Competency Model provides a common framework and a detailed, validated method to define and develop the profession. It also provides the focal point for prioritizing lifelong learning. Educators can use the model to

- assess learners' needs by measuring current capabilities against the competencies and AOEs

- take stock of learners' interest in enhancing their development
- evaluate existing course offerings to see what aspects of the model they are developing
- update existing course offerings to include broader coverage of AOEs and competencies
- plan an entire curriculum for the profession
- develop specific course offerings to improve performance in particular competencies or AOEs
- guide students' development paths by evaluating individual development needs
- create measures, tests, and indicators that evaluate performance in the competencies and AOEs
- evaluate faculty expertise.

Warner Burke, professor of psychology and education at Teacher's College, Columbia University, remarked that the ASTD Competency Model is extremely valuable to educators: "The model clearly points the way for additional scholar-practice work, and it helps us to assess workplace learning in a much more focused and relevant way. As a result, our research efforts can be applied much more effectively."

What's Next

It's time to take the WLP profession to the next level. Chapter 7 serves as a call to action to do just that.

Chapter 7

It's Up to Each Person

The ASTD Competency Model was created with the input of more than 2,000 thought leaders, experts, and practitioners in the profession. It was developed *by* the profession *for* the profession. The model provides a common language and framework of competencies that define the field—both for today and for years to come—more sharply than ever before.

The WLP profession has long championed learning and self-development as an indispensable part of the adult learning experience. The ASTD Competency Model provides members of the profession with a blueprint for continuous learning.

The model also provides a blueprint for success. It enables practitioners to increase their relevance in the business world by sharing accountability for and adding value to their organization's performance. Being viewed as professionals who link learning efforts to organizational goals and strategies in a meaningful way has never been more critical. It is time for members of the profession to ensure that all learning efforts achieve measurable results that align with business strategy.

According to Tony Bingham, CEO of ASTD, "This study is an important step toward mobilizing all parts of this dynamic profession behind a common goal of maximizing the talent in organizations and leveraging that talent to meaningfully and measurably improve business performance."

Although many WLP practitioners are already viewed as important strategic partners by top executives and line managers, not all are. The profession has the potential to make an even greater difference and to have a more enduring impact in years to come.

It is up to each one of us. The competency model will have little value unless it is used to develop professionals further and drive performance higher. The challenge to the profession is clear: Embrace learning and invest in personal development and growth. Doing so will push the profession to higher levels of expertise and respect, enabling practitioners to make a measurable difference in helping their customers, clients, and colleagues in the years ahead.

Appendix A

Competency Model Dictionary

A CD-ROM, containing a PDF of this competency dictionary, is included with this book. The CD is meant as a companion piece to *ASTD Competency Study: Mapping the Future.*

Table of Contents

ASTD Competency Model

Roles

R oles are broad areas of responsibility within the WLP profession that require a certain combination of competencies and AOEs to perform effectively. They are described in sensible, intuitive, and everyday language. Like competencies, roles can be demonstrated in the context of most WLP jobs. Roles are not the same as job titles; they are much more fluid, depending on the application or the project. For the WLP professional, playing the roles is analogous to maintaining a collection of hats—when the situation calls for it, the professional slips out of one role and "puts on" another.

This study has identified four unique roles within the workplace learning and performance profession: Learning Strategist, Business Partner, Project Manager, and Professional Specialist. These four roles are further defined as follows:

- **Learning Strategist**—Determines how workplace learning and performance improvement can best be leveraged to achieve long-term business success and add value to meet organizational needs; leads in the planning and implementation of learning and performance improvement strategies that support the organization's strategic direction and that are based on an analysis of the effectiveness of existing learning and performance-improvement strategies.

- **Business Partner**—Applies business and industry knowledge to partner with the client in identifying workplace performance-improvement opportunities; evaluates possible solutions and recommends solutions that will have a positive impact on performance; gains client agreement and commitment to the proposed solutions and collaboratively develops an overall implementation strategy that includes evaluating impact on business performance; uses appropriate interpersonal styles and communication methods to build effective long-term relationships with the client.

- **Project Manager**—Plans, resources, and monitors the effective delivery of learning and performance solutions in a way that supports the overall business venture; communicates purpose, ensures effective execution of an implementation plan, removes barriers, ensures adequate support, and follows up.

- **Professional Specialist**—Designs, develops, delivers, or evaluates learning and performance solutions; maintains and applies an in-depth working knowledge in any one or more of the workplace learning and performance specialty areas of expertise, including Career Planning and Talent Management, Coaching, Delivering Training, Designing Learning, Facilitating Organizational Change, Improving Human Performance, Managing Organizational Knowledge, Managing the Learning Function, and Measuring and Evaluating.

Table A-1 indicates the competencies that an individual who is effective in each of the roles would likely exhibit. This table is provided as an illustrative example only. Further research is required to confirm the linkages, which are beyond the scope of this report.

Table A-1. Competencies linked to roles.				
	Learning Strategist	Business Partner	Project Manager	Professional Specialist
Analyzing Needs and Proposing Solutions	X	X	X	X
Applying Business Acumen	X	X		
Building Trust	X	X	X	X
Communicating Effectively	X	X	X	X
Demonstrating Adaptability	X	X	X	X
Driving Results	X	X	X	
Influencing Stakeholders	X	X		
Leveraging Diversity	X	X	X	X
Modeling Personal Development	X	X	X	X
Networking and Partnering	X	X	X	
Planning and Implementing Assignments		X	X	X
Thinking Strategically	X	X		

Competencies

Competencies are clusters of skills, knowledge, abilities, and behaviors required for job success. Managers need to know about competencies to make appropriate personnel decisions and guide employees' performance. Employees need to know about competencies because they provide a roadmap of how to succeed on the job.

The study identified the following set of competencies—presented below in alphabetical order—that are considered important and necessary for the majority of individuals in the workplace learning and performance profession:

- Analyzing Needs and Proposing Solutions
- Applying Business Acumen
- Building Trust
- Communicating Effectively
- Demonstrating Adaptability
- Driving Results
- Influencing Stakeholders
- Leveraging Diversity
- Modeling Personal Development
- Networking and Partnering
- Planning and Implementing Assignments
- Thinking Strategically.

These competencies are grouped into clusters (Business/Management, Interpersonal, and Personal) to facilitate understanding. The competencies are listed alphabetically under each cluster.

Business/Management Competencies

- Analyzing Needs and Proposing Solutions
- Applying Business Acumen
- Driving Results
- Planning and Implementing Assignments
- Thinking Strategically.

Interpersonal Competencies

- Building Trust
- Communicating Effectively
- Influencing Stakeholders
- Leveraging Diversity
- Networking and Partnering.

Personal Competencies

- Demonstrating Adaptability
- Modeling Personal Development.

Business/Management Competencies

....

Analyzing Needs and Proposing Solutions

Identifying and understanding business issues and client needs, problems, and opportunities; comparing data from different sources to draw conclusions; using effective approaches for choosing a course of action or developing appropriate solutions; taking action that is consistent with available facts, constraints, and probable consequences.

....

Key Actions

Gathers information about client needs—Collects information to better understand client needs, issues, problems, and opportunities; reviews organizational information and human performance outcomes; studies organizational systems to better understand the factors affecting performance; integrates information from a variety of sources; asks internal and external partners for input and insight.

Diagnoses learning and performance issues—Uses research methods to isolate the causes of human learning and performance problems; proposes theories to understand and explain the factors affecting performance; detects trends, associations, and cause-effect relationships.

Generates multiple alternatives—Gathers information about best practices; thinks expansively and brainstorms multiple approaches; generates relevant options for addressing problems/opportunities and achieving desired outcomes; maintains a database or bank of possible solutions and their effectiveness.

Searches for innovative solutions—Challenges paradigms and looks for innovative alternatives; draws upon diverse sources for ideas and inspiration in creative problem-solving activities.

Chooses appropriate solution(s)—Formulates clear decision criteria; evaluates options by considering implications, risks, feasibility, and consequences on the client system and on other parts of the organization; prioritizes and chooses an effective option.

Recognizes impact—Considers the implications of learning and performance decisions, solutions, and strategies in other contexts; makes decisions using a broad range of knowledge that extends beyond the limitations of the organization and its immediate needs.

Proposes solution(s)—Recommends a plan or process for making changes; clearly explains rationale for the recommended solution and how it will address the performance gap or opportunity.

Applying Business Acumen

Understanding the organization's business model and financial goals; utilizing economic, financial, and organizational data to build and document the business case for investing in workplace learning and performance solutions; using business terminology when communicating with others.

Key Actions

Understands the business—Understands the organization's business model and competitive position in the marketplace; understands how the business is leveraging core competencies for growth and profitability; understands the value proposition to external customers.

Understands business operations—Understands the organization's structure, systems, functions, and business processes; understands how the organization operates, including its planning processes, decision-making channels, and information management systems; understands how products and services are developed, sold, and delivered to customers.

Applies financial data—Understands financial goals and interprets financial data related to business success measures, such as a balanced scorecard; accurately reads and understands the implications of balance sheets, graphs, charts, tables, etc.; performs quantitative calculations in building a business case, preparing budgets, evaluating program impact, and calculating return-on-investment (ROI).

Uses business terminology to gain credibility—Translates learning and performance jargon into business terminology that stakeholders will understand and respect; speaks the language of the business when applying professional expertise.

Recognizes business priorities—Tracks the changing needs and expectations of external customers; identifies links between internal demands and external needs; works to understand the business priorities of internal clients and how the learning function could help them achieve greater success.

Creates a value proposition—Establishes the link between business needs and specific solutions; documents how solutions will achieve targeted business results; identifies outcomes that will result from implementing learning and performance solutions; creates a compelling business case.

Advances the learning and performance business agenda—Understands how decisions are made in the organizational structure and how power is exercised; recognizes key stakeholders and their priorities; leverages understanding of politics across business units and decision makers; presents and defends the business value of learning and performance solutions.

Driving Results

Identifying opportunities for improvement and setting well-defined goals related to learning and performance solutions; orchestrating efforts and measuring progress; striving to achieve goals and produce exceptional results.

Key Actions

Targets improvement opportunities—Systematically evaluates business opportunities and targets those with the greatest potential for impacting results; identifies opportunities to improve organizational performance; continually seeks new ways of leveraging human performance to improve business results.

Establishes goals and objectives—Sets stretch goals to encourage higher performance; establishes SMART (specific, measurable, achievable, realistic, time-bound) objectives to achieve reliable business results.

Orchestrates effort to achieve results—Mobilizes additional resources as needed and works tenaciously to achieve stretch goals.

Overcomes obstacles—Identifies obstacles to achieving the organization's strategy; anticipates and overcomes barriers; prevents irrelevant issues or distractions from interfering with timely completion of important tasks.

Provides courageous leadership—Takes a stand and follows through with actions that support business objectives, even when those actions may be unpopular.

Planning and Implementing Assignments

Developing action plans, obtaining resources, and completing assignments in a timely manner to ensure that workplace learning and performance goals are achieved.

Key Actions

Establishes parameters and forecasts outcomes—Identifies critical project parameters along with potential needs and trends that may affect success; agrees to action and commits resources based on careful consideration of possible future events.

Uses planning tools to create project plans—Uses planning tools such as Gantt charts, risk analysis, and roles/responsibility matrices to create a practical action plan; identifies critical activities and assignments along with less-critical tasks; adjusts the project plan and priorities as needed.

Manages budget—Calculates projected costs and develops budget; monitors expenses relative to budgeted costs; adjusts spending and resource allocation as new challenges arise.

Determines tasks and resources—Determines project requirements by breaking them down into tasks and identifying types of equipment, materials, and persons needed.

Plans for contingencies—Proactively identifies potential problems and creates contingency plans or work-arounds to implement if problems occur.

Mobilizes resources—Takes advantage of available resources (people, processes, departments, and tools) to complete work efficiently; coordinates with internal and external partners.

Manages time—Allocates appropriate amounts of time for completing own and others' work; avoids scheduling conflicts; develops timelines and milestones and stays focused on achieving them.

Tracks progress and ensures completion—Monitors progress to ensure projects are completed on time and efficiently; follows up with individuals as needed to check progress; regularly communicates with stakeholders to ensure that promised goals have been achieved; identifies what is working well along with problems and obstacles; makes course corrections during the project.

Thinking Strategically

Understanding internal and external factors that impact learning and performance in organizations; keeping abreast of trends and anticipating opportunities to add value to the business; operating from a systems perspective in developing learning and performance strategies and building alignment with business strategies.

Key Actions

Understands external factors impacting learning and performance—Understands the political, economic, sociological, cultural, and global factors that can affect an organization's performance in the marketplace; understands the context within which workplace learning and performance takes place in terms of government actions, legal requirements, and wider societal needs.

Understands the organizational context for learning and performance—Understands how learning and performance contribute to organizational success; understands the ways in which "people development" is implemented by line managers and functional specialists; understands how different aspects of HR and HRD are integrated with each other, the business strategy, and organizational structures.

Recognizes and acts on emerging opportunities—Anticipates how trends may impact and shape the learning and performance industry; scans and monitors new developments in other fields and industries; shows curiosity about the business and challenges assumptions; seeks inspiration from different perspectives in constructing future scenarios; frames options for the learning and performance function to add value to the business.

Builds strategic alignment—Contributes to the development and refinement of the organization's vision, goals, and strategies with a focus on human capital; integrates and synthesizes other viewpoints to build alignment.

Develops learning and performance strategies—Develops both short- and long-term workplace learning and performance strategies that support the organization's strategic direction; generates options to achieve a long-range strategic goal or vision.

Operates from a systems perspective—Views the organization as a dynamic system; recognizes the need to understand and integrate interconnected elements; sees the big picture and complex relationships; recognizes patterns and broad implications of issues; balances long-term strategic goals with short-term priorities when making decisions.

Interpersonal Competencies

Building Trust

Interacting with others in a way that gives them confidence in one's intentions and those of the organization.

Key Actions

Operates with integrity—Demonstrates honesty and behaves according to ethical principles; ensures that words and actions are consistent; walks the talk; behaves dependably across situations.

Discloses position—Shares thoughts, feelings, and rationale so that others understand positions and policies.

Maintains confidentiality—Keeps private or sensitive information about others confidential.

Leads by example—Serves as a role model for the organization's values; takes responsibility for delivering on commitments; gives proper credit to others; acknowledges own mistakes rather than blaming others.

Treats people fairly—Treats all stakeholders with dignity, respect, and fairness; listens to others without prejudging; objectively considers others' ideas and opinions, even when they conflict with prescribed policies, procedures, or commonly held beliefs; champions the perspectives of different partners even in the face of resistance; engages in effective conflict resolution.

Ensures compliance with legal, ethical, and regulatory requirements—Ensures that processes and results comply with relevant legal, ethical, and regulatory requirements; monitors compliance and creates reports if needed.

Communicating Effectively

Expressing thoughts, feelings, and ideas in a clear, concise, and compelling manner in both individual and group situations; actively listening to others; adjusting style to capture the attention of the audience; developing and deploying targeted communication strategies that inform and build support.

Key Actions

Develops and deploys effective communication strategies—Creates plans for communicating and leveraging information; employs diverse media to summarize and convey results.

Delivers clear messages—Uses appropriate vocabulary; understands the material and demonstrates command of the topic; logically and simply conveys ideas.

Presents with impact—Speaks with appropriate pace and inflection; conveys an air of confidence, ease, and enthusiasm; uses congruent nonverbal communication; uses visual aids to enhance understanding of the content.

Adjusts message content and delivery—Monitors audience reactions and adopts alternative strategies to improve overall impact; presents own message in different ways to enhance understanding; responds appropriately to questions and feedback.

Demonstrates active listening—Listens to others, interprets their message correctly; checks understanding; acknowledges different viewpoints.

Invites dialogue—Engages others in dialogue by using appropriate questioning techniques and involving others in conversations about things that matter; encourages people to express their hopes and fears; welcomes feedback.

Creates clear written communication—Writes clearly and understandably; sequences information in a logical manner to aid understanding; avoids jargon or technical words; uses a tone and format suggested by the topic and audience.

Masters multiple communication methods—Selects communication media and methods based on the needs of the recipients; adapts to virtual work situations involving remote workers who may use a range of communication styles and methods.

Influencing Stakeholders

Selling the value of learning or the recommended solution as a way of improving organizational performance; gaining commitment to solutions that will improve individual, team, and organizational performance.

Key Actions

Analyzes stakeholder perspectives—Identifies key stakeholders, analyzes likely reactions, and determines how to address their unique needs and preferences.

Establishes a marketing strategy—Develops a strategy for presenting the business case and proposed solution; plans how to leverage supportive factors and overcome or minimize barriers; prepares a communication campaign.

Communicates a strong value proposition—Helps listeners understand how the proposed learning and performance solution will achieve targeted business results; provides convincing rationale based on the business case.

Builds energy and support—Encourages collaboration from people representing different levels and functions; invites people to participate in the decision-making process to obtain good input, create buy-in, and ensure understanding of the resulting decisions.

Gains commitment to the solution—Uses various influencing techniques to win support for the proposed learning solution; makes persuasive arguments, handles objections, negotiates key points, and summarizes outcomes; gains agreement to implement a solution or take partnership-oriented action.

Leveraging Diversity

Appreciating and leveraging the capabilities, insights, and ideas of all individuals; working effectively with individuals having diverse styles, abilities, motivations, and backgrounds (including cultural differences).

Key Actions

Conveys respect for different perspectives—Shows respect both verbally and nonverbally by making decisions and taking actions that reflect appreciation for cultural concerns and expectations; displays empathy for other points of view; maintains a nonjudgmental attitude.

Expands own awareness—Establishes relationships with people from other cultures, countries, races, and backgrounds; learns more about differences in social norms, decision-making approaches, and preferences; encourages dialogue that promotes acceptance of different opinions; continually examines own biases and behaviors to avoid stereotypical responses.

Adapts behavior to accommodate others—Modifies behavior to help make others feel comfortable and accepted; accommodates different learning styles and preferences by providing a mixture of learning and performance solutions.

Champions diversity—Advocates the value of diversity; takes actions to increase diversity in the workplace (for example, by recruiting and developing people from varied backgrounds and cultures); confronts racist, sexist, or inappropriate behavior by others; challenges exclusionary organizational practices.

Leverages diverse contributions—Solicits ideas and opinions from diverse individuals having varied backgrounds; utilizes different perspectives to generate more possibilities in creative problem solving; maximizes effectiveness by assigning work that capitalizes on people's unique talents and abilities.

Accommodates global differences—Demonstrates awareness of differences in business customs and cultural practices in various parts of the world; recognizes that people face additional comprehension and communication challenges when working in a second language; adjusts processes and expectations to facilitate their full participation in meetings, conference calls, workshops, etc.

Networking and Partnering

Developing and using a network of collaborative relationships with internal and external contacts to leverage the workplace learning and performance strategy in a way that facilitates the accomplishment of business results.

Key Actions

Networks with others—Proactively builds a personal network of individuals and groups inside and outside of the organization who can provide quick advice or solutions; includes influential people (such as senior leaders, department heads, external vendors/suppliers) and learning and performance experts.

Benchmarks and shares best practices—Maintains contacts with others outside of the organization to learn from their experiences and share best practices in workplace learning and performance; regularly learns from others in the profession through personal communications and conference interactions.

Establishes common goals—Places priority on organization goals and finding ways for partners to work together for the common goal; establishes common ground with workplace learning and performance goals to facilitate cooperation.

Develops partnering relationships—Establishes strong interpersonal relationships by staying in close contact with key individuals and working cooperatively; helps others feel valued and appreciated by monitoring their needs and exchanging occasional favors (for example, providing a sounding board to test proposals or learn what's happening in other parts of the industry).

Generates new collaborative possibilities—Seeks and expands on original ideas, enhances others' ideas, and contributes own ideas about the issues at hand; gains clarity about own thinking; expands options for future collaboration.

Personal Competencies

Demonstrating Adaptability

Maintaining effectiveness when experiencing major changes in work tasks, the work environment, or conditions affecting the organization (for example, economic, political, cultural, or technological); remaining open to new people, thoughts, and approaches; adjusting effectively to work within new work structures, processes, requirements, or cultures.

Key Actions

Seeks to understand changes—Seeks to understand changes in work tasks, situations, and environment as well as the logic or basis for change; actively seeks information about new work situations and withholds judgment.

Approaches change positively—Treats changes as opportunities for learning or growth; focuses on the beneficial aspects of change; speaks positively and advocates the change when it helps promote organizational goals and strategy.

Remains open to different ideas and approaches—Thinks expansively by remaining open to different lines of thought and approaches; readily tries new and different approaches in changing situations.

Adjusts behavior—Quickly modifies behavior to deal effectively with changes in the work environment; acquires new knowledge or skills to deal with the change; does not persist with ineffective behaviors; shows resiliency and maintains effectiveness even in the face of uncertainty or ambiguity.

Adapts to handle implementation challenges—Effectively handles global, cultural, economic, social, and political challenges to the effective implementation of learning and performance solutions; works to overcome barriers and deal constructively with nontraditional or challenging situations.

Modeling Personal Development

Actively identifying new areas for one's own personal learning; regularly creating and taking advantage of learning opportunities; applying newly gained knowledge and skill on the job.

Key Actions

Models self-mastery in learning—Serves as a role model for taking responsibility to manage own learning and development; seeks feedback and uses other sources of information to identify appropriate areas for personal improvement; targets learning needs and takes action.

Seeks learning activities—Demonstrates motivation for continuous learning; identifies and participates in appropriate learning activities (for example, courses, reading, self-study, coaching, experiential learning) that help fulfill personal learning needs; values and pursues lifelong learning.

Takes risks in learning—Puts self in unfamiliar or uncomfortable situations in order to learn; asks questions at the risk of appearing foolish; takes on challenging or unfamiliar assignments.

Maximizes learning opportunities—Actively participates in learning activities in a way that makes the most of the learning experience (for example, takes notes, asks questions, critically analyzes information, keeps potential applications in mind, does required tasks); remains open to unplanned learning opportunities, such as coaching from others.

Applies new knowledge or skill—Puts new knowledge, understanding, or skill to practical use on the job; furthers learning through trial and error in practicing new approaches and behaviors.

Maintains professional knowledge—Pursues learning in professional area(s) of expertise; monitors new developments in the industry to identify new areas of learning; seeks knowledge in areas beyond current area(s) of expertise; stays abreast of learning trends and emerging learning technologies; maintains memberships in relevant professional associations; attends professional meetings and conferences; reads journals and professional publications.

Areas of Expertise

Professional areas of expertise are the specific technical and professional skills and knowledge required for success in WLP specialty areas. Think of AOEs as the knowledge and skills an individual must have above and beyond the foundational competencies. In order to function effectively in a given AOE, a person must display a blend of the appropriate foundational competencies and unique technical/professional skills and knowledge. An individual may have expertise in one or more of the following specialty areas (listed alphabetically below):

- Career Planning and Talent Management
- Coaching
- Delivering Training
- Designing Learning
- Facilitating Organizational Change
- Improving Human Performance
- Managing Organizational Knowledge
- Managing the Learning Function
- Measuring and Evaluating.

Career Planning and Talent Management

Ensuring that employees have the right skills to meet the strategic challenges of the organization; assuring the alignment of individual career planning and organization talent management processes to achieve an optimal match between individual and organizational needs; promoting individual growth and organizational renewal.

Key Knowledge

- Workforce planning approaches
- Succession and replacement-planning approaches
- Job analysis tools and procedures
- Career development theories and approaches
- Individual and organizational assessment tools, including assessment center methodologies
- Ethical standards and legal issues in career counseling and organizational restructuring
- Career counseling approaches
- Coaching and mentoring approaches
- Performance consulting approaches
- Managerial and leadership development best practices
- Performance management systems and techniques
- Approaches to maximize workplace diversity
- Resources for career exploration and lifelong learning.

Key Actions

Creates success profiles—Analyzes key jobs and roles to determine the knowledge and skills necessary for high-performance; develops success profiles for key roles in organization.

Identifies capability requirements—Works with internal clients/stakeholders to determine the mix and level of capability required by the organization to meet current needs and future strategic objectives.

Coordinates succession planning—Works with internal clients/stakeholders to design, develop, and implement succession and replacement-planning programs to fill key positions now and in the future; aligns succession plans with business needs and goals.

Implements individual and organizational assessments—Provides tools and resources to assess individual and organizational strengths, development needs, and limits; aggregates data to evaluate organizational capabilities; offers tools for the enhancement of skills and potential; arranges for psychological tests to be administered by qualified professionals.

Facilitates the career development planning process—Provides support for identifying skills, aptitudes, interests, values, accomplishments, career goals, and realistic opportunities, and for preparing development plans; orchestrates challenging assignments that build skill, knowledge, confidence, and credibility; monitors alignment between success profiles and individual development plans.

Organizes delivery of developmental resources—Provides flexible access to multiple vehicles for developing talent (such as training, e-learning, coaching, mentoring), job rotation, and expatriate assignments; selects and manages training suppliers and consultants; monitors delivery of solutions to ensure successful implementation; plans and manages resources to ensure adequate coverage.

Initiates strategic development programs—Develops programs to meet high-priority needs (for example, establishing diversity initiatives, arranging cross-cultural training for expatriates, involving high-potentials in action learning projects, setting up a career center to retrain displaced workers).

Equips managers to develop their people—Educates managers on their role to help people develop while performing their jobs; provides various tools (such as e-learning, workshops, skill practice sessions) to help managers learn how to coach; helps managers offer a more enriching work environment that engages the excitement and contribution of employees; holds managers accountable for developing talent; encourages employees to take responsibility for their own development.

Promotes high-performance workplaces—Advocates the recognition and reward of high performance; actively pursues appropriate recognition, rewards, and resources for high-performing individuals and groups; balances the investment in high-performance talent with the responsibility for providing learning and growth opportunities to all employees.

Administers performance management systems—Works with internal customers to design, develop, implement, and administer performance management systems; ensures that individual goals, behavior, and performance are linked to strategic organizational objectives; evaluates human performance improvement.

Conducts career counseling sessions—Contracts with clients for service delivery; facilitates setting career and life goals; provides individual and group counseling sessions to enhance career skills and employability potential; offers guidance on preparing job-search materials and on interviewing; provides ongoing consultation to facilitate introspection about expectations and potential job fit.

Facilitates career transitions—Works with internal customers to provide consulting services and tools to facilitate individual career transitions such as onboarding, job changes, promotions, or outplacement; prepares managers to carry out employee terminations.

Sample Outputs

- Stakeholder analysis
- Succession plan
- Talent reviews
- 360° feedback programs
- Acceleration pools (identification of high-potential talent)
- Individual development plans (IDPs)
- Action learning programs
- Leadership development programs
- Mentoring programs
- Internal career reappraisal programs
- Team alignment programs
- Diversity initiatives
- Evaluation data (such as a satisfaction survey, a measurement of what's changed, return-on-investment).

Coaching

Using an interactive process to help individuals and organizations develop more rapidly and produce more satisfying results; improving others' ability to set goals, take action, make better decisions, and make full use of their natural strengths.

PLEASE NOTE: *This information is based on the ICF (International Coach Federation) Code of Ethics and the ICF Core Coaching Competencies. A full text of these documents can be found at ICF's Website, www.coachfederation.org.*

Key Knowledge

- Standards of conduct
- Ethical guidelines
- Core coaching competencies (setting the foundation, co-creating the relationship, communicating effectively, facilitating learning and results).

Key Actions

Meets ethical guidelines and professional standards—Understands coaching ethics and standards and applies them appropriately in all coaching situations.

Establishes coaching agreement—Understands what is required in the specific coaching interaction and comes to agreement with the prospective and new client about the coaching process and relationship; identifies how the coaching goals link to enhanced business performance.

Establishes trust and intimacy with the client—Creates a safe, supportive environment that produces ongoing mutual respect and trust.

Displays coaching presence—Is fully conscious (that is, engaged) and creates a spontaneous relationship with the client, employing a style that is open, flexible, and confident.

Demonstrates active listening—Focuses completely on what the client is saying, and not saying, to understand the meaning of what is said in the context of the client's desires and to support client self-expression.

Asks powerful questions—Asks questions that reveal the information needed for maximum benefit to the coaching relationship and the client.

Uses direct communication—Communicates effectively during coaching sessions and uses language that has the greatest positive impact on the client.

Creates awareness—Integrates and accurately evaluates multiple sources of information and makes interpretations that help the client gain awareness and thereby achieve agreed-upon results.

Designs actions—Creates with the client, opportunities for ongoing learning—during coaching and in work/life situations—and for taking new actions that will most effectively lead to agreed-upon coaching results.

Develops goals and plans—Develops and maintains an effective coaching plan with the client.

Manages progress and accountability—Holds attention on what is important for the client and leaves responsibility with the client to take action.

Sample Outputs

- Evaluation component (such as a satisfaction survey, a measurement of what's changed, return-on-investment)
- Individual development plans (IDPs)
- Progress reporting
- Initial contract
- Skill set around assessment.

Delivering Training

Delivering learning solutions (for example, courses, guided experience) in a manner that both engages the learner and produces desired outcomes; managing and responding to learner needs; ensuring that the learning solution is made available or delivered in a timely and effective manner.

Key Knowledge

- Adult learning theories and techniques
- Instructional design theory and methods
- Various instructional methods, such as lecture, discussion, practical exercises, etc.
- Various delivery options/media, such as online learning, classroom training, print media, etc.
- Existing learning technologies and support systems, such as collaborative learning software, learning management systems, and authoring tools
- Emerging learning technologies and support systems
- Presentation techniques and tools
- Organizational work environment and systems, including learning delivery channels
- Individual learning styles, such as audiovisual
- Cultural differences in learning styles, communication, classroom behavior, etc.
- Own personal learning preferences, such as a preference for lecture or experience-based learning, and how that impacts delivery capabilities
- Tools for determining learning preferences, such as a preference for lecture or experience-based learning, etc.
- Familiarity with content being taught and how the solution addresses the need (that is, context)
- Legal and ethical issues relevant for delivering training.

Key Actions

Prepares for training delivery—Reviews participant and facilitator materials prior to delivery; gathers information about the participants and their characteristics; tailors examples and analogies to ensure relevance to participants, etc.

Aligns learning solutions with course objectives and learner needs—Monitors needs and learning preferences of users/participants to ensure that the learning solutions meet learner and course objectives; responds to feedback from learners and makes adjustments or enhancements to the learning solution based on feedback.

Conveys objectives—Ensures users/participants are informed of the goals and purpose of the learning solution prior to the training and have a realistic understanding of what the solution can accomplish.

Delivers various learning methodologies—Uses various learning delivery mechanisms/options and selected methodologies that could include a combination of lectures, role plays, simulations, technology-delivered training or e-learning, learning technology support tools, etc.; follows facilitator materials to ensure effective and consistent delivery.

Facilitates learning—Varies delivery style to fit the audience; adapts to the needs of learners and adjusts curriculum as needed; presents information in a logical sequence; uses appropriate visual aids; listens and responds to questions and objections; manages group dynamics; manages time on learning topics.

Encourages participation and builds learner motivation—Uses techniques and skills prior to and during delivery to actively engage all participants in the learning experience; adapts own style to different learner and group styles; makes effort to bring in passive or resistant participants; creates excitement and commitment to the learning experience; engages learners by providing opportunities for participation and experimentation in the learning process; values and capitalizes on participant diversity to maximize learning.

Establishes credibility as instructor—Demonstrates understanding of course content; uses appropriate terminology and relevant business examples; provides useful information when responding to questions; helps participants apply learning to on-the-job situations.

Manages the learning environment—Schedules events and users/participants; selects facilities conducive to learning; prepares agenda/learning objectives in advance; presents and organizes materials and multimedia equipment; arranges room and equipment for optimal learning; provides materials; ensures access to and supplies resources for learning users/participants; provides for breaks/refreshments.

Delivers constructive feedback—Provides behavioral feedback on learners' performance during or after the learning experience; maintains or enhances learners' self-esteem; supports feedback with specific examples of behavior and possible alternatives for improving performance; provides a balance of positive and constructive/developmental feedback; creates opportunities for self-awareness and insight.

Creates a positive learning climate—Establishes a learning environment where learners feel safe to try new skills and behaviors, where individual differences are respected, and where confidentiality is supported; ensures an appropriate level of management and organizational support; personally models behavior that is consistent with the goals of the program.

Ensures learning outcomes—Ensures the learning objectives are met; integrates or embeds appropriate performance support and assessment techniques to check learners' understanding and to ensure skill and/or knowledge acquisition, on-the-job application, and intended business results.

Evaluates solutions—Monitors the impact of learning solutions to ensure their effectiveness; summarizes and communicates evaluation results.

Sample Outputs

- Report of learning usage
- Evaluation report of impact of learning solution
- Return-on-investment report
- Delivery schedule
- Learner feedback
- Presentations of materials
- Facilitations of learning events
- Facilitations of group discussions
- Feedback to learners
- Action plans for knowledge transfer.

Designing Learning

Designing, creating, and developing learning interventions to meet needs; analyzing and selecting the most appropriate strategy, methodologies, and technologies to maximize the learning experience and impact.

PLEASE NOTE: *This information is based in part on the ibstpi (International Board of Standards for Training, Performance and Instruction) competency study for instructional design competencies:* The Standards *(R. Richey, D.C. Fields, & M. Foxon, with R.C. Roberts, T. Spannaus, & J.M. Spector, [2001]).*

Key Knowledge

- Cognition and adult learning theory
- Instructional design theory and process
- Various instructional methods, such as lecture, discussion, practical exercise, feedback, etc.
- Various delivery options/media, such as online learning, classroom training, print media, etc.
- Job/Task analysis and competency modeling
- Content knowledge or techniques to elicit content from subject matter experts
- Assessment methods and formats, such as multiple choice, hands-on, open-ended response, etc.
- Learning technologies and support systems, such as collaborative learning software, learning management systems, and authoring tools
- New and emerging learning technologies and support systems
- Business strategy, drivers, or needs associated with possible learning interventions
- Research methods, including information scanning, data gathering, and analysis
- Individual, group, and organizational differences that influence learning, such as cultural norms/values, cognitive abilities, learning preferences, previous experience, and motivation
- Legal and ethical issues related to designing learning, including accessibility and intellectual property
- Differences between e-learning and traditional courses and their implications
- Design of information displays, access, and resources.

Key Actions

Applies cognition and adult learning theory—Incorporates sound principles of current cognition and adult learning theory to the practice of instructional design.

Collaborates with others—Builds partnerships and relationships among the participants in a learning design project and establishes sign-off and approval processes for each step of the design process.

Conducts a needs assessment—Identifies target population characteristics and characteristics of the environment; gathers and evaluates resources and information, analyzes findings, and incorporates or synthesizes information into the design and development process; identifies anticipated constraints or problems affecting design success or failure, such as equipment deficiencies, lack of support, etc.; defines basic outcomes of the learning intervention to solve the problem or meet the opportunity.

Designs a curriculum or program—Uses a variety of techniques for determining instructional content of curriculum or program; creates or partners with others to plan and design the curriculum or program.

Creates designs or specifications for instructional material—Selects, modifies, or creates an appropriate design or specification document and development model or plan for a given project; identifies and documents measurable learning objectives; selects and uses a variety of techniques to define, structure, and sequence the instructional content and strategies; designs instructional content to reflect an understanding of the diversity of learners or groups of learners; builds into the design on-the-job application tools and learning aids.

Analyzes and selects technologies—Analyzes the characteristics, benefits, pros/cons, etc., associated with existing and emerging technologies, including e-learning options and their possible application in an instructional environment; considers e-learning options, such as extended books and lectures, extended community, extended expert access, simulations, and embedded help; selects technologies based on a needs-driven approach in order to accomplish learning goals and objectives.

Integrates technology options—Integrates existing and emerging technologies to achieve learning goals; integrates new material and technologies with existing learning resources to produce an effective blended solution.

Develops instructional materials—Selects or modifies existing instructional materials or develops new instructional materials; conducts review of materials with appropriate parties, such as subject matter experts, design team, and the target audience; creates logical learning units/objects as appropriate; designs or builds assets (such as role plays, self-assessment tests, job aids) to support the learning experience and meet objectives as appropriate; develops instructional content to reflect an understanding of the diversity of learners or groups of learners.

Evaluates learning design—Proactively identifies appropriate evaluation techniques and applies them, such as summative and formative evaluation, four levels of evaluation, usability testing, etc.; conducts appropriate test and revision cycles to assess and test the learning design solution and its impact; assesses whether the learning design solution produces positive results, such as a change in learner attitude, skill, knowledge, and behavior.

Manages others—Directs, assigns, or manages the work of others on the design team to accomplish project goals and objectives.

Manages and implements projects—Identifies sponsors or champions to help ensure successful project implementation; sources work, budgets, plans and organizes, manages activities, and executes learning design projects.

Sample Outputs

- Business case for learning solution
- Templates for instructional materials
- Learning objects
- Learning objectives
- Design specifications
- Content outline
- Storyboards or scripts
- Job aids
- Instructor/Facilitator materials
- Evaluation tools.

Facilitating Organizational Change

Leading, managing, and facilitating change within organizations.

PLEASE NOTE: *This information is based in part on the 20th edition of the* Organization Change and Development Competency Effort. *Contributors include ODN (Organization Development Network), ODI (Organization Development Institute), the Academy of Management Directors of OD university programs, Twin Cities ASTD Chapter, and more than 3,000 individuals from around the world. R. Sullivan, W.J. Rothwell, and C. Worley coordinated the ongoing research.*

Key Knowledge

- Systems thinking and open systems theory, such as the organization is an open system influenced by the external environment
- Chaos and complexity theory
- Appreciative inquiry theory
- Action research theory
- Organizational systems and culture, including political dynamics in organizational settings
- Change theory and change models, including change strategy, infrastructures and roles, change process, types of change, how people change, human reactions, pacing strategies, and impact analysis
- Process thinking and design
- Communication theory
- Engagement practices to build critical mass
- Diversity and inclusion, including managing differences
- Motivation theory, including empowerment and rewards
- Mindset/Mental models and their influence on behavior and performance.

Key Actions

Establishes sponsorship and ownership for change—Clarifies case for change and desired outcomes; facilitates client sponsorship of expected outcomes; engages stakeholders to build critical mass of support.

Creates a contract for change—Helps clients contract for change, clarify outcomes, and establish realistic expectations for change; identifies boundaries for change; clarifies relationships, roles, and ethical parameters; creates conditions for success.

Conducts diagnostic assessments—Determines what data are needed to clarify issues, including stakeholder expectations; collects information to pinpoint initial steps; diagnoses problems as well as perceptions favoring change; assesses current reality against business/organizational strategy and desired outcomes to define change efforts needed; identifies formal and informal power networks; establishes design requirements for future state.

Provides feedback—Prepares clients/stakeholders for receiving the results of data gathering and diagnosis; provides feedback to people in position to influence course corrections on change strategy; articulates what is happening and what needs to happen in a complex system; builds an impetus to support change.

Facilitates strategic planning for change—Facilitates creation of overall change strategy with sponsor and key change leaders; clarifies what must change and how to minimize the human impact and optimize buy-in; helps identify all technical, organizational, cultural, and people-related change initiatives; shapes the best process and conditions to accomplish results; designs appropriate change process plans to be time efficient and responsive to human needs.

Builds involvement—Involves people to raise awareness and gathers input on the best course of action; helps clients and change leaders build involvement and ownership in the change process; helps clients create a communication plan that generates buy-in and commitment; facilitates effective two-way communications to ensure understanding, commitment, and behavior change.

Supports the change intervention—Helps clients design, assess impacts, plan, and implement the change effort and strategy; identifies innovative ways to structure the system; creates new approaches or models of programs as appropriate; offers advice and support for managing complex projects as needed; refines change strategy; supports learning and course correction.

Integrates change into organizational culture—Creates shared mindset in support of change; ensures alignment of all systems, policies, and processes of the organization to match and support the change; ensures integration and mastery of change effort so that it becomes the norm.

Manages consequences—Creates strategy to reduce human trauma; manages reactions to the change intervention and the unanticipated consequences of the change; surfaces and resolves conflict; helps clients overcome resistance; influences those who react negatively to support the change interventions.

Evaluates change results—Facilitates information-sharing during the intervention to ensure that results match intentions; collects information about the impact of change; communicates results and best change practices to interested stakeholders.

Models mastery of leading change—Understands own role as facilitator, including personal stake in the change; demonstrates self-awareness of how others perceive the change agent; makes personal changes that support the desired future; recognizes when the change agent's skills are no longer required and acts appropriately; leaves the client system able to proceed with future changes when appropriate.

Sample Outputs

- Change needs assessment
- Case for change
- Change strategy
- Design requirements
- New models of programs or approaches
- Change plan, including outcomes, expectations, milestone events, and appropriate pacing
- Strategy for involving stakeholders and engaging employees
- Communication strategy
- Documented contingency plans
- Project reports
- Metrics to measure change outcomes and change process
- Evaluation report documenting impact of change and best practices.

Improving Human Performance

Applying a systematic process of discovering and analyzing human performance gaps; planning for future improvements in human performance; designing and developing cost-effective and ethically justifiable solutions to close performance gaps; partnering with the customer when identifying the opportunity and the solution; implementing the solution; monitoring the change; evaluating the results.

PLEASE NOTE: *This information is based in part on* ASTD Models for Human Performance Improvement *(Rothwell; 1996 and 2000).*

Key Knowledge

- Human performance improvement discipline, including the mindset, vision, culture, and goals
- Performance analysis and organizational analysis
- Front-end analysis
- Approaches for selecting performance-improvement solutions
- Change management theory
- Measurement and evaluation methods and theory
- Facilitation methods
- Project management tools and techniques
- Evaluation methods and theory
- Communication channel, informal network, and alliance
- Group dynamics process
- Human Performance Improvement model
- Systems thinking and theory
- Questioning techniques.

Key Actions

Analyzes systems—Identifies inputs, throughputs, and outputs of a subsystem, system, or supra-system, and applies that information to improve human performance; realizes the implications of solutions on many parts of an organization, a process, or an individual, and takes steps to address any side effects of human performance improvement solutions; evaluates how organizational politics may affect performance.

Conducts performance analysis—Compares actual and ideal performance; identifies performance gaps or opportunities; identifies who is affected by the performance gap and conditions that affect performance.

Conducts cause analysis—Identifies the root causes of a past, present, or future performance gap; clarifies the real problem underlying the need for the performance improvement; breaks down the components of a larger whole; examines work environments for·issues or characteristics that affect human performance.

Gathers data—Gathers pertinent information to stimulate insight in individuals and groups through use of general research methods, interviews, and other data-gathering techniques.

Identifies the customer—Identifies the real customer rather than just assuming the individual requesting help is the customer.

Incorporates customer/stakeholder needs—Partners with the customer/stakeholder to clarify needs, business goals, and objectives; agrees on desired results and gains agreement on how those results can be achieved efficiently and effectively.

75

Selects solutions—Selects appropriate human performance improvement solutions that address the root cause(s) of performance gaps rather than symptoms or side effects.

Manages and implements projects—Identifies sponsors or champions to help ensure successful project implementation; sources work, budgets, plans and organizes, manages, and executes complex performance improvement projects.

Builds and sustains relationships—Builds credibility and trust with the client based on knowledge and understanding of the business; partners and collaborates with the client on an ongoing basis to maintain a sustained business relationship.

Evaluates results against organizational goals—Assesses how well the results of a human performance improvement solution match intentions; ensures that goals are converted effectively into actions to close existing or pending performance gaps; obtains results despite conflicting priorities, lack of resources, or ambiguity; links human performance improvement to organizational goals.

Monitors change—Monitors the human performance improvement solutions as they are being implemented; assesses how changing conditions inside and outside the organization affect or impact the solution.

Uses feedback skills—Collects information about performance and feeds it back clearly, specifically, and on a timely basis to affected individuals or groups.

Sample Outputs

- Analysis data and recommendations
- Data collection tools
- Action plans
- Solution designs
- Evaluation reports
- List of root causes
- Performance metrics
- Solutions specifications
- Risk-management reports
- Systems flowcharts
- Project reports
- Project plans
- Evaluation plans.

Managing Organizational Knowledge

Serving as a catalyst and visionary for knowledge sharing; developing and championing a plan for transforming the organization into a knowledge-creating and knowledge-sharing entity; initiating, driving, and integrating the organization's knowledge management efforts.

Key Knowledge

- Knowledge management concepts, philosophy, and theory
- Knowledge management history and best practices
- Appreciation of the range of activities and initiatives used to establish an environment in which knowledge is effectively created, shared, and used to increase competitive advantage and customer satisfaction
- Technology and how it enables the knowledge-sharing and learning process
- Understanding the primary processes of the business; experience with the organization's operations and business tools
- Strategies and approaches to managing culture change
- Information architecture
- Database management
- Business process analysis
- Systems analysis and design
- Adult learning theory
- After Action Review (AAR) methodology.

Key Actions

Champions knowledge management (KM)—Develops the KM vision and strategy, ensuring that it integrates with the organization's business strategy; helps the organization understand the concept and value of effective knowledge creation, sharing, and reuse; assists senior management in building and communicating personal commitment and advocacy for KM; actively promotes the knowledge agenda.

Benchmarks KM best practices and lessons learned—Examines the experiences of other organizations in developing effective and innovative KM solutions and approaches as appropriate; learns from other organizations that leverage their knowledge resources effectively.

Creates a KM infrastructure—Oversees the creation and development of the organization's knowledge architecture and infrastructure; establishes processes, policies, and procedures for capturing, organizing, using, and maintaining intellectual capital; provides standardized tools and templates to make knowledge sharing easier; builds bridges between information systems, training, human resources, and the business units in support of the knowledge network.

Leverages technology—Assesses, selects, and applies current and emerging information, learning tools, and technologies to support work-related learning and knowledge development.

Manages information life cycle—Manages the life cycle of information from its creation or acquisition through its destruction, including organizing, categorizing, cataloging, classifying, disseminating, etc.

Encourages collaboration—Examines the design of the workplace and social environments to encourage and facilitate knowledge creation, sharing, and innovation; creates knowledge-content activities to contribute to or manage the capture, sharing, and retention activities, such as the After Action Review process; facilitates knowledge-oriented connections, coordination, and communication activities across organizational boundaries.

Establishes a knowledge culture—Fosters a culture of acceptance of knowledge management; cultivates or supports innovation; helps break down the barriers between business units, functions, geographic locations, hierarchical layers, etc., to motivate people to share and use knowledge.

Designs and implements KM solutions—Assesses the specific knowledge needs of business processes and workers within those processes; identifies knowledge objects that can be handled in the information system; integrates KM into employees' job activities, into key processes, and across communities of practice.

Transforms knowledge into learning—Assesses organizational learning capabilities; maximizes learning at the individual level; uses knowledge capture and sharing as a way to enhance organization-wide learning; facilitates drawing tacit knowledge from experts (knowledge that experts have but cannot articulate) and makes it explicit knowledge so that others can learn it.

Evaluates KM success—Assesses the effectiveness of KM strategies, practices, and initiatives; measures benefits and progress against goals; establishes metrics to measure how well the organization leverages its intellectual assets.

Sample Outputs

- Strategy/Plan for knowledge sharing within the organization
- Analysis, summaries, and reports of knowledge
- Systems (such as online) providing access to information
- Records of knowledge management use (such as frequency of system access).

Managing the Learning Function

Providing leadership in developing human capital to execute the organization's strategy; planning, organizing, monitoring, and adjusting activities associated with the administration of workplace learning and performance.

Key Knowledge

- Needs assessment methodologies and learning needs identification
- Adult learning theory
- Learning design theory
- Learning technologies, such as distance learning, e-learning options
- Learning information systems
- Marketplace resources (that is, learning and performance products and services; capabilities of potential supplier partners)
- Basic understanding of all learning, development, and performance programs being administered
- Budgeting, accounting, and financial management
- Principles of management
- Project-planning tools and processes
- Communication and influencing strategies and tools
- Human resource systems and how they integrate, such as recruitment, selection, compensation, performance management, reward management
- Organization's business model, drivers, and competitive position in the industry
- External systems (that is, political, economic, sociological, cultural, and global factors that can affect the organization's performance in the marketplace)
- Legal, regulatory, and ethical requirements pertaining to managing the learning function, such as federal/state/local employment laws like the ADA or EEOC Uniform Guidelines.

Key Actions

Establishes a vision—Creates a compelling picture of how the learning function can improve the performance of the business and enable execution of the organization's strategy; partners with business unit leaders to advocate for improving human performance through the learning function.

Establishes strategies—Develops long-range learning, development, and human performance strategies to implement the vision; understands what drives the business and determines how the learning function can best add value.

Implements action plans—Converts the workplace learning and performance strategies into action plans; balances or reconciles strategy with real-life constraints of the workplace; creates a reasonable timeline that conforms to the expectations of customers/stakeholders.

Develops and monitors the budget—Ensures budgets are prepared and followed; prepares budget or project reports on a schedule or an as-needed basis.

Manages staff—Recruits, selects, and manages people in the learning function; assigns roles, responsibilities, and projects; conducts performance appraisals and makes compensation decisions.

Models leadership in developing people—Serves as a role model in own function; provides coaching and mentoring to individuals or groups; supports continuous learning and staff development that enhances performance; builds team capabilities in effectively partnering with line functions to improve business performance.

Manages external resources—Identifies which training-related activities can be outsourced; determines external resources available for providing learning and performance solutions; selects the most appropriate resources for the solution being provided; negotiates and manages contracts with external partners; maintains contact with external partners to ensure effective delivery.

Ensures compliance with legal, ethical, and regulatory requirements—Ensures that all delivery complies with relevant legal, ethical, and regulatory requirements; monitors compliance and creates reports as needed.

Sample Outputs

- Learning and development proposals
- Requests for proposals (RFPs)
- Human resource strategy white papers
- Status reports for managers (on development of their staffs)
- Fulfilled learning plans
- Improved human and organizational performance.

Measuring and Evaluating

Gathering data to answer specific questions regarding the value or impact of learning and performance solutions; focusing on the impact of individual programs and creating overall measures of system effectiveness; leveraging findings to increase effectiveness and provide recommendations for change.

Key Knowledge

- Statistical theory and methods
- Research design
- Analysis methods, such as cost-benefit analysis, return-on-investment, etc.
- Interpretation and reporting of data
- Theories and types of evaluation, such as four levels of evaluation.

Key Actions

Identifies customer expectations—Works with customers or stakeholders to determine why they are interested in measurement and what they hope to accomplish with the results; clearly defines research questions, expectations, resources available, and desired outcomes of the measurement project; manages unrealistic expectations.

Selects or designs appropriate strategies, research design, and measures—Uses customer questions and expectations to guide the selection or design of appropriate strategies, research designs, and quantitative and qualitative measurement tools; employs a variety of measures and methods to reduce bias and ensure objective conclusions; identifies appropriate sample sizes, data-tracking methods, and reporting formats; balances practical implications of rigor, effort, real-life constraints, and objectivity to create a workable approach.

Communicates and gains support for the measurement and evaluation plan—Summarizes measurement approach into a clear plan that can be communicated to customers and stakeholders; communicates timelines and roles/responsibilities, and identifies other project management needs; gains buy-in for the plan and ensures that all parties understand the approach and their responsibilities.

Manages data collection—Ensures that all data collection methods are applied consistently and objectively; monitors ongoing data collection to ensure that assumptions required for statistical inference are being met; manages and documents data in a format that can be adequately manipulated during the analysis process (such as spreadsheets).

Analyzes and interprets data—Creates descriptive and inferential summaries of data in a format that can be readily understood and communicated; adheres to rules of statistical analysis to reduce bias and provide adequate support for conclusions; uses a process of creative inquiry to fully explore the data and all of its possible implications and meaning.

Reports conclusions and makes recommendations based on findings—Provides data summaries in a format that can be readily understood and interpreted by customers and stakeholders (potentially multiple summaries); organizes information in a way that directly responds to research questions; bases recommendations and conclusions on sound analysis methods; clarifies customer questions and the meaning of the data.

Sample Outputs

- Research or measurement plans (includes data collection plan, project plan, communication plan, implementation plan)
- Reports that summarize the impact of the solution in question (includes statistical analyses, charts, tables, interpretation of data)
- Recommendations for change based on the data
- Measurement tools (such as surveys, focus group protocol)
- Scorecard.

Appendix B

A History of the ASTD Competency Models

A Short History Lesson About the Models

ASTD has sponsored six studies of practitioner roles and competencies. These studies all attempted to identify what roles should be fulfilled and what competencies successful practitioners should demonstrate.

By looking back on these six works, WLP practitioners can see how the field has gradually moved away from a single area of focus (that is, training) to an emphasis on learning as a means to an end: improving human performance. These studies have built a framework for thinking about the field and have driven professional development and education curricula to prepare people to break into the profession or advance in it.

The studies in this ASTD tradition include:

- *ASTD Models for Workplace Learning and Performance* (Rothwell, Sanders, & Soper, 1999)
- *ASTD Models for Learning Technologies* (Piskurich & Sanders, 1998)
- *ASTD Models for Human Performance Improvement* (Rothwell, 1996 and 2000)
- *Models for HRD Practice* (McLagan, 1989)
- *Models for Excellence* (McLagan & McCullough, 1983)
- *A Study of Professional Training and Development Roles and Competencies* (Pinto & Walker, 1978).

Each study reflects a major shift in thinking about the competencies essential for professionals' success. And each study is regarded as an evolutionary—and sometimes revolutionary—shift in defining the field and establishing expectations for practitioners and stakeholders. A brief description of each study follows.

1999: *ASTD Models for Workplace Learning and Performance*

ASTD Models for Workplace Learning and Performance was guided by two areas of inquiry:

- What competencies do practitioners, senior practitioners, and line managers perceive as currently required for success in the field of workplace learning and performance?
- What competencies do practitioners, senior practitioners, and line managers perceive as being required for success in the field of workplace learning and performance in five years?

The 1999 report defined workplace learning and performance as "the integrated use of learning and other interventions for the purpose of improving individual and organizational performance. It uses a systematic process of analyzing performance and responding to individual, group, and organizational needs. WLP creates positive, progressive change within organizations by balancing human, ethical, technological, and operational considerations" (Rothwell, Sanders, & Soper, 1999, p. 121).

As in the earlier ASTD studies, this report defined *roles* as "a grouping of competencies targeted to meet specific expectations of a job or function. Roles are not synonymous with job titles" (Rothwell et al., 1999, p. xv). The report identified seven workplace learning and performance roles (Rothwell et al., pp. xv-xvi) as follows:

- The *manager* plans, organizes, schedules, monitors, and leads the work of individuals and groups to attain desired results; facilitates the strategic plan; ensures that workplace learning and performance is aligned with organizational needs and plans; and ensures the accomplishment of the administrative requirements of the function.

- The *analyst* isolates and troubleshoots the causes of human performance gaps or identifies areas for human performance improvement.
- The *intervention selector* chooses appropriate interventions to address root causes of human performance gaps.
- The *intervention designer and developer* creates learning and other interventions that help to address the specific root causes of human performance gaps. Some examples of the work of the intervention designer and developer include serving as instructional designer, media specialist, materials developer, process engineer, ergonomics engineer, instructional writer, and compensation analyst.
- The *intervention implementor* ensures the appropriate and effective implementation of desired interventions to address the specific root causes of human performance gaps. Some examples of the work of the intervention implementor include serving as administrator, instructor, organization development practitioner, career development specialist, process redesign consultant, workspace designer, compensation specialist, and facilitator.
- The *change leader* inspires the workforce to embrace the change, creates a direction for the change effort, helps the organization's workforce adapt to the change, and ensures the continuous monitoring and guiding of interventions in ways consistent with stakeholders' desired results.
- The *evaluator* assesses the impact of the interventions and provides participants and stakeholders with information on how well the interventions were implemented and received by the employees.

The study used a three-fold methodology that compared perceptions of a cross-cultural mix of practitioners, senior practitioners, and line managers to identify 52 *competencies*, understood in ASTD's tradition to mean "an area of knowledge or skill that is critical for producing key outputs . . . international capabilities that people bring to their jobs" (McLagan, 1989, p. 77). These competencies were classified into six groupings:

- *analytical competencies*—the creation of new understandings or methods through the synthesis of multiple ideas, processes, and data
- *technical competencies*—the understanding and application of existing knowledge or processes
- *leadership competencies*—influencing, enabling, or inspiring others to act
- *business competencies*—the understanding of organizations as systems and of the processes, decision criteria, and issues that businesses face
- *interpersonal competencies*—the understanding and application of methods that produce effective interactions between people and groups
- *technological competencies*—the understanding and appropriate application of current, new, or emerging technologies.

Comparing Competencies: 1999 and 2004

The 12 competencies in the 2004 ASTD model represent a natural evolution of the 1999 ASTD research. As mentioned earlier, the 1999 study rated 52 competencies, which included some technical activities related to specific WLP positions. Some of the top-ranked competencies identified in the 1999 report (see table B-1) included content related to specific areas of expertise (for example, training delivery). Not all of these competencies are appropriate for professionals working in other areas of expertise (such as knowledge management). For example, although facilitation was a top 10 competency in the 1999 report, most of the survey respondents were experts in training delivery and design. It's not surprising, then, that facilitation was rated so highly.

In the 2004 study, analysts began with a list of competencies from the 1999 study. This list was expanded, revised, and later validated by more than 2,000 WLP professionals. Several of the top ten competencies from the 1999 model are now a part of the areas of expertise in the current model. Table B-1 shows how the top ten 1999 competencies and their definitions are addressed in the 2004 model.

Table B-1. Comparing the top 10 1999 competencies with the 2004 model.

Top-Ranked 1999 Competencies . . .	. . . Compared with the 2004 ASTD Model
1. **Leadership**—Leading, influencing, and coaching others to help them achieve desired results.	**Note:** "Leadership" is often a loosely defined concept with many different elements. Components of leadership appear in many of the foundational competencies in the 2004 model. Leadership is also addressed in the AOE, Managing the Learning Function. • **Thinking Strategically** • **Influencing Stakeholders** • **Analyzing Needs and Proposing Solutions.**
2. **Analytical Thinking**—Clarifying complex issues by breaking them down into meaningful components and synthesizing related items.	**Analyzing Needs and Proposing Solutions**—Identifying and understanding business issues and client needs, problems, and opportunities; comparing data from different sources to draw conclusions; using effective approaches for choosing a course of action or developing appropriate solutions; taking action that is consistent with available facts, constraints, and probable consequences.
3. **Competency Identification**—Identifying the skills, knowledge, and attitudes required to perform work.	**Note:** This competency is a specialty area that is addressed in the AOE Career Planning and Talent Management. **Analyzing Needs and Proposing Solutions**—See definition above.
4. **Communication**—Applying effective verbal, nonverbal, and written communication methods to achieve desired results.	**Communicating Effectively**—Expressing thoughts, feelings, and ideas in a clear, concise, and compelling manner in both individual and group situations; actively listening to others; adjusting style to capture the attention of the audience; developing and deploying targeted communication strategies that inform and build support.
5. **Interpersonal Relationship Building**—Effectively interacting with others in order to produce meaningful outcomes.	**Networking and Partnering**—Developing and using a network of collaborative relationships with internal and external contacts to leverage the workplace learning and performance strategy in a way that facilitates the accomplishment of business results.
6. **Performance Gap Analysis**—Performing "front-end analysis" by comparing actual and ideal performance levels in the workplace; identifying opportunities and strategies for performance improvement.	**Note:** This competency is addressed in the AOE Improving Human Performance. **Analyzing Needs and Proposing Solutions**—See definition above.
7. **Intervention Selection**—Selecting performance improvement strategies that address the root cause(s) of performance gaps rather than treat symptoms or side effects.	**Analyzing Needs and Proposing Solutions**—See definition above.
8. **Identification of Critical Business Issues**—Determining key business issues and forces for change and applying that knowledge to performance improvement strategies.	**Applying Business Acumen**—Understanding the organization's business model and financial goals; utilizing economic, financial, and organizational data to build and document the business case for investing in workplace learning and performance solutions; using business terminology when communicating with others.
9. **Facilitation**—Helping others to discover new insights.	**Note:** This is a specialty competency that is addressed in the AOE Delivering Training. **Communicating Effectively**—See definition above. **Influencing Stakeholders**—Selling the value of learning or the recommended solution as a way of improving organizational performance; gaining commitment to solutions that will improve individual, team, and organizational performance.
10. **Ability to See the "Big Picture"**—Identifying trends and patterns that are outside the normal paradigm of the organization.	**Thinking Strategically**—Understanding internal and external factors that impact learning and performance in organizations; keeping abreast of trends and anticipating opportunities to add value to the business; operating from a systems perspective in developing learning and performance strategies and building alignment with business strategies.

1998: *ASTD Models for Learning Technologies*

The 1998 report, *ASTD Models for Learning Technologies*, examines the roles, competencies, and work outputs that HRD professionals need to implement learning technologies within their organizations. (HRD is defined in the 1989 study.) It also provides a classification system that relates instructional methods (for example, lectures, role plays, and simulations) to presentation methods (for example, computer-based training, electronic performance support systems, multimedia, and video) and distribution methods (for example, audiotape, CD-ROM, Internet, and videotape; Piskurich & Sanders, 1998). Although this work enhanced understanding of the issues surrounding learning technologies, it did not intend to describe the larger field within which training resides.

1996: *ASTD Models for Human Performance Improvement*

ASTD Models for Human Performance Improvement (Rothwell, 1996) explores the roles, competencies, and outputs that human performance improvement professionals (performance consultants) need to effect meaningful changes within organizations. Based on expert opinion, the report emphasizes that human performance improvement (HPI) is a process, not a discipline. Another example of a process is instructional systems design (ISD), which practitioners use to analyze, design, develop, deliver, and evaluate training programs. ISD, in its many forms, encompasses the logical steps that a training professional can follow to create effective training. A host of disciplines within WLP (for example, human resource development, human resources, performance consulting, ergonomic design, and line management) carry out the HPI process. The title *HPI practitioner* represents anyone who sets out to solve business problems using the HPI model.

ASTD Models for Human Performance Improvement does the following:

- Defines HPI as "the systematic process of discovering and analyzing important human performance gaps, planning for future improvements in human performance, designing and developing cost-effective, ethically justifiable interventions to close the performance gaps, implementing the interventions, and evaluating the financial and nonfinancial results" (p. 79).

- Lists trends in the following five key areas "that are expected to influence and change the way we work" (Brock in Rothwell, 1996, p. 11): performance, business, learning, organizational structure, and technology.

- Describes 14 terminal outputs of HPI work and 81 enabling outputs. A *terminal output* is "a final outcome directly associated with a particular role"; an *enabling output* is "a specific output associated with the demonstration of a particular competency" (p. 79).

- Pinpoints 15 core and 38 supporting competencies of HPI.

- Summarizes four roles of HPI professionals: analyst, intervention specialist, change manager, and evaluator.

- Identifies 16 key ethical issues affecting HPI work (Dean in Rothwell, 1996).

A key point of the 1996 study is that everyone in organizational settings plays an important part in improving performance and contributes to enhanced organizational competitiveness. Practitioners, line managers, employees, and others may perform HPI work; HRD professionals are not its sole practitioners. A second key point is that no one individual can play all the roles and master all the competencies described in *ASTD Models for Human Performance Improvement*. Instead, the report supplies a menu of options for doing HPI work.

1989: *Models for HRD Practice*

The immediate predecessor of *ASTD Models for Human Performance Improvement* is the report titled *Models for HRD Practice* (McLagan, 1989). This study was groundbreaking because it expanded the profession beyond training and development to include career development and organization development. Naming the field *human resource development*, the report:

- defines HRD as "the integrated use of training and development, organization development, and career development to improve individual, group, and organizational effectiveness" (p. 7)

- positions HRD within the larger human resource field through a human resource wheel encompassing 11 activity areas:

  —training and development
  —organization development
  —career development
  —organization/job design
  —human resource planning
  —performance management systems
  —selection and staffing
  —compensation and benefits
  —employee assistance
  —union/labor relations
  —human resource research and information systems (p. 18).

- lists 13 future forces affecting HRD
- describes 74 outputs of HRD work
- identifies quality requirements for each output
- pinpoints 35 competencies for HRD
- identifies key ethical issues affecting HRD work
- summarizes 11 roles of HRD professionals:

  —researcher
  —marketer
  —organization change agent
  —needs analyst
  —program designer
  —HRD materials developer
  —instructor/facilitator
  —individual career development advisor
  —administrator
  —evaluator
  —HRD manager.

The 1989 study was an expansion of the 1983 study, which focused on training and development alone.

1983: *Models for Excellence*

Models for Excellence was launched in 1981 when Patricia McLagan carried out a series of studies focused on training and development (T&D) and the trainer's role. This study represented the first modern attempt to define training and development. It also established the

format for all the competency model studies that have come since. In the 1983 report, the format for T&D managers and practitioners included the following:

- a human resource "wheel"
- a definition of T&D
- a list of 34 future forces expected to affect the T&D field
- 15 T&D roles
- 102 critical outputs for the T&D field
- 31 T&D competencies
- four role clusters
- a matrix of 15 roles/31 competencies (McLagan & McCullough, 1983).

1978: *A Study of Professional Training and Development Roles and Competencies*

Pinto and Walker conducted *A Study of Professional Training and Development Roles and Competencies*, the first published effort sponsored by ASTD, in 1978. Their goal was to investigate what training and development professionals really do. Its objective was to "define the basic skills, knowledge, understanding, and other attributes required for professionals for effective performance of training and development activities" (p. 2).

To that end, six panels of ASTD chapter members and the Professional Development Committee of ASTD reviewed the study questionnaire. The final study questionnaires, containing 92 multiple-choice items, were mailed to more than 14,000 ASTD members in the United States, Canada, and Mexico, with another 500 going to members outside North America. A total of 2,790 usable questionnaires were returned to achieve a nearly 20 percent response rate.

The ensuing report revealed the following major areas for T&D practitioners (Pinto & Walker, 1978):

- analyzing and diagnosing needs
- determining appropriate training approaches
- designing and developing programs
- developing material resources
- managing internal resources
- managing external resources
- developing and counseling individuals
- preparing job- or performance-related training

- conducting classroom training
- developing group and organization
- conducting research on training
- managing working relationships with managers and clients
- managing the training and development function
- managing professional self-development.

What's Next

All the ASTD competency studies used a systematic approach to determine what it takes to be a successful practitioner in the field. The approach used in the study is described in appendix C.

For copies of any of the reports mentioned in this section, contact ASTD.

Purpose

The purpose of this research project is to develop a valid and defensible list of roles, competencies, and AOEs relevant for practitioners in the workplace learning and performance profession. The roles, competencies, and AOEs should be comprehensive enough to address both emerging trends and current responsibilities. As such, the final model was developed based on a multi-perspective and multi-method approach to avoid bias from any one information source. The methodology used to develop the ASTD Competency Model adheres to guidelines set forth by the National Organization for Competency Assurance (NOCA).

Although the model is intended to be comprehensive, it must be specific enough to identify particular knowledge areas, skills, and abilities. The model's ultimate effectiveness is defined by how it will be used (for example, guiding development, providing selection criteria, determining certification standards). The combination of roles, competencies, and AOEs must be valuable for achieving a particular goal or set of outcomes. All the competencies in the model are important for success, but an individual might perform only one role or multiple roles, depending on his or her position and tenure in the profession. If practitioners effectively display all the competencies in the model, they should be considered highly valuable for organizations that hope to promote learning and development in the workplace.

Competency-Based Certification

ASTD's Board of Directors has approved efforts to explore development of a certification program at the time of writing. For the model to serve as the foundation for certification, it must specifically address the knowledge, skills, and abilities necessary for individuals who fulfill various roles associated with promoting learning and performance in the workplace. The model presented in this report will serve as the foundation for developing a certification framework.

Design and implementation of a certification process will require more in-depth analysis of the model and specific delineation of the exact skills and knowledge areas required for success. Depending on the job, organization, and individual, the specific combination of learning and performance roles and competencies required for effectiveness can vary. Therefore, the actual certification process/program might take a variety of forms and specializations.

Approach

To create the ASTD Competency Model, analysts began with three primary sources of data and progressed through an extensive review and validation process. The phases delineated in figure C-1 outline the basic development process.

Phase I: Needs Assessment and Data Collection

1. Expert Interviews

Analysts gathered information from job incumbents, executives, and thought leaders regarding current and future job competency/role requirements. This approach focused on the strategic direction of jobs in the industry and job-specific activities. Most of the information obtained through interviews was collected

Figure C-1. Process used to create the ASTD Competency Model.

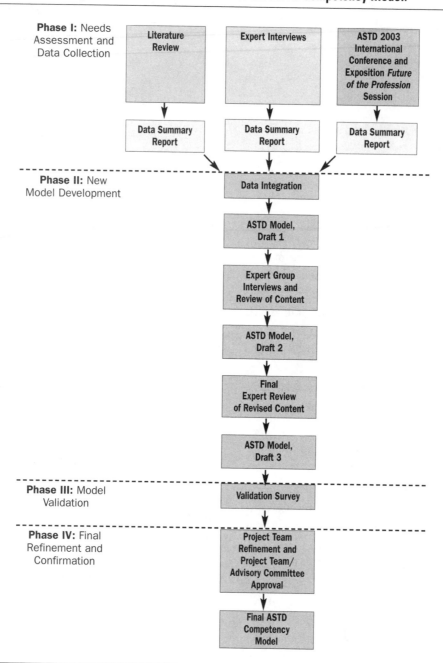

Phase I: Needs Assessment and Data Collection

- Literature Review → Data Summary Report
- Expert Interviews → Data Summary Report
- ASTD 2003 International Conference and Exposition *Future of the Profession* Session → Data Summary Report

Phase II: New Model Development

- Data Integration
- ASTD Model, Draft 1
- Expert Group Interviews and Review of Content
- ASTD Model, Draft 2
- Final Expert Review of Revised Content
- ASTD Model, Draft 3

Phase III: Model Validation

- Validation Survey

Phase IV: Final Refinement and Confirmation

- Project Team Refinement and Project Team/ Advisory Committee Approval
- Final ASTD Competency Model

during the ASTD 2003 International Conference and Exposition. Analysts used a series of predetermined questions to interview nearly 50 WLP professionals (the demographics of these individuals can be found in appendix D). Additional phone interviews were conducted with people who were unable to attend the conference. Questions used in the interview were created and refined by members of the project team. The questions were designed to elicit both conceptual and practical ideas regarding the future trends and current competencies. During the interviews, analysts asked the following questions:

- **Future Trends**
  —What key trends or drivers will have the greatest impact or influence on WLP work and competencies over the next few years?

—What effect will this have on what professionals need to know or be able to do?

- **Competencies.** Interviewees were shown the list of WLP roles and competencies from the 1999 study. They received these verbal instructions: "This list of roles and competencies is from an ASTD study conducted in 1999. Please take a moment to review these pages and let me know if you have any questions." Then they were asked a series of questions:

  —To what extent do you think this model accurately reflects the profession? What's missing? What needs to be changed?

  —What would be the impact on organizations if workplace learning and performance professionals embraced these changing roles and competencies you've described?

  —What would be the impact on workplace learning and performance professionals themselves?

Criteria for Selecting Interviewees. Thirty-one interviewees were recognized thought leaders in the industry. ASTD and DDI targeted conference attendees who have published and spoken extensively in their areas of expertise. Analysts ensured that interviewees selected were from a cross section of industries, positions, nationalities, and AOEs when possible. Analysts made special efforts to conduct some interviews with professionals from outside the United States. Appendix D lists the demographics of the targeted interviewees. In addition, 17 interviews were conducted randomly with International Conference and Exposition attendees who expressed an interest in the study. Analysts felt that a mix of recognized industry experts and practitioners would provide a balance of information that was both comprehensive and practical.

Analysis and Integration. Analysts transcribed all interviewee comments and created an aggregate report with demographic information. All answers to interview questions were systematically summarized into a spreadsheet. Comments were read several times, coded, and clustered into themes. Sample competencies derived from the interviews included Business Acumen, Evaluation, Change Leader, and Performance Consulting.

2. ASTD 2003 International Conference and Exposition *Future of the Profession* Session

One of the sessions during the conference focused on future directions for the WLP profession. This session involved invited attendees who represented numerous thought leaders and a broad cross section of the profession. To ensure accurate representation, analysts collected demographic information from all participants (see appendix D). Jim Haudan, of Root Learning Inc., and Rebecca Ray, of American Skandia, used learning maps in facilitating the session, which addressed a specific set of questions about the past and future state of WLP roles. Questions posed in the session included:

- What will the future of training and learning look like?
- What will the role of training and learning leaders look like?
- What will be the necessary competencies of the future leaders of learning?
- What will we as individuals do? What must we do differently? What can we do now?

Analysis and Integration. Information from the session was transcribed into an aggregate report with demographic information. All comments were read several times, coded, and integrated into a summary report. The report contained the primary trends, emerging roles, and competencies needed in the profession. Some of the key themes identified in the session included the idea that training and learning will

- focus on improving results
- be aligned with the business strategy
- meet individual learners' needs.

Competencies for success included Adaptability, Strategic Decision Making, and Building Strategic Working Relationships.

3. Literature Review

Analysts conducted a search of current international publications, studies, and Websites to ensure an adequate analysis of competencies, roles, and AOEs. Two review lists were created—a list of trends and a compilation of preliminary competencies. After each resource was read, it was summarized into a set of key findings relative to WLP competencies and trends. These summaries were used to produce an integrated analysis of common findings. Competencies identified during this initial analysis included Visionary and Strategic Leadership, Global Acumen, Driving for Results, and Information Monitoring. The following is a brief sample of sources:

- Chartered Institute of Personnel and Development (CIPD)
- International Board of Standards for Training, Performance and Instruction (ibstpi)
- International Society for Performance Improvement (ISPI)
- Society for Human Resource Management (SHRM)
- World Federation of Personnel Management Associations (WFPMA).

Phase II: New Model Development
1. Data Integration to Create ASTD Model, Draft 1

Pulling together information from all available resources (literature, interviews, *Future of the Profession* session), analysts identified the revised competencies and roles that best represented the data. The process used to draft the model was based on both qualitative (that is, interpretation of comments) and quantitative (for example, frequency of mention in publications) judgments. The roles and competencies were defined as fully and as clearly as possible using a paragraph definition and sample outputs. The competencies included a brief definition and key actions. To ensure continuity with past research, analysts cross-referenced competencies and roles from the 1999 ASTD model (see appendix B) and documented any changes in content. Additionally, individual competencies in the new model were specifically mapped to at least five other major competency studies. This approach ensured that the competencies identified were derived from consistent and powerful trends in findings across multiple publications and studies. In some cases, analysts leveraged existing competency models from other associations or organizations, such as the International Coach Federation, to create the key actions and knowledge

areas for certain AOEs. Where appropriate, the links to these preexisting models are documented in appendix A and on the CD-ROM that accompanies this report.

2. Expert Group Interviews and Review of Content

Focus groups or interviews were conducted with industry experts and practitioners to review and refine the competency/role model and the certification model.

- **Competencies/Roles.** Analysts scheduled five 2 1/2-hour group interviews involving approximately 30 individuals who reviewed the existing model content. Participants were given 30 minutes to review the model for accuracy and provide suggestions for refinement in their areas of content expertise. A list of these experts and others who contributed to the study can be found in appendix E.
  —*Selection Criteria*—Participants were identified based on their past participation in the interview process (Phase I) and recognition in the industry as thought leaders (see criteria in Phase I). Analysts drew heavily from ASTD members, including chapter leaders, international contingents, board members, and other influential members. Six groups were formed based on their expertise in the following subject areas:
  - technology and knowledge management
  - training and instructional design
  - organization development
  - coaching and career development
  - learning as a business strategy
  - performance and return-on-investment (ROI)
  - general practitioners—this special group of participants covered a range of specializations and included a range of tenure in the industry (minimum of three years).
  —*Interview questions included:*
  - **Part I: Core Competencies and Roles**
    1. In terms of coverage, does the list of competencies address all of the major competencies required for individuals

working in the WLP profession? If not, what competencies should be added? What is your rationale?

2. Should any of the competencies be removed, combined, or subdivided? Are they sufficiently discrete? What should be changed? Why?

3. What specific edits do you have for competency titles, definitions, or key actions? (Interviewers reviewed each competency individually and asked for input.)

4. Does the list of roles cover all of the major roles for the WLP profession? If not, what roles should be added?

5. Should any of the roles be removed, combined, or subdivided? Are they sufficiently discrete? What should be changed? Why?

6. What specific edits do you have for role titles, definitions, or representative actions? (Interviewers reviewed each role individually and asked for input.)

- **Part II: Areas of Expertise**

7. In terms of coverage, does the list of areas of expertise (AOEs) address most of the major specialty areas in the WLP profession? If not, what AOE should be added? What is your rationale?

8. Should any of the AOEs be removed, combined, or subdivided? Are they sufficiently discrete? What should be changed? Why?

9. In this session we are asking you to specifically address only one or two of the AOEs in which you have expertise. For the AOE you are reviewing, what specific edits do you have for titles, definitions, key knowledge areas, or key actions?
   a. Suggestions for rewording definition?
   b. Key Knowledge
      —Is it covering everything?
      —What needs to be added?

—What needs to be deleted?
—What needs to be edited?
   c. Key Actions
      —Is it covering everything?
      —What needs to be added?
      —What needs to be deleted?
      —What needs to be edited?

10. Are you aware of any existing certification programs for this AOE? What are they?

11. Outputs are products or services that an individual delivers to others (for example, a written plan and a report would be considered outputs). Please list some of the common outputs that an individual would produce when using knowledge and skills associated with this professional/technical competency.

- **Creation of ASTD Model, Draft 2.** Based on input from the Phase II focus groups and interviews, analysts developed a more refined and detailed model. Definitions, key actions, and outputs were expanded and adjusted to reflect expert opinions.

3. Final Expert Review of Revised Content and Creation of ASTD Model, Draft 3

A final round of reviews allowed experts to confirm revisions, make enhancements, and ensure that the competency model was ready for wide-scale validation. Each component of the model was discussed in a group setting with experts involved, as appropriate, to review all changes and edits. At this point, modifications were small and focused primarily on the AOEs. The final model was based on a balance of past research, expert opinion, and practicality. Draft 3 of the model submitted for wide-scale validation by survey in Phase III was almost identical to the final model presented in this report.

Phase III: Model Validation

During this phase, analysts administered a survey on a Website using third-party software. The content of the survey mirrored the structure of the ASTD competency model and its content. Survey questions were designed to address a list of critical questions posed by the research team (such as relative importance of the competencies and time spent performing each AOE).

1. Survey Content

All survey participants were asked to rate roles and competencies in terms of importance and frequency of use. Participants were also asked to indicate their primary area of expertise and then were prompted to rate content appropriate for their expertise. The competencies, roles, and AOEs presented in the survey were based on the refined model developed from the information gathered in Phases I and II. Copies of the survey are on file at ASTD.

2. Selection Criteria

The primary source of respondents was ASTD's membership database. However, to ensure that the resulting model has application outside the membership, analysts worked with other professional organizations to publicize and promote participation in the survey. The final list of partner groups included members of:

- AITD—Australian Institute of Training and Development
- ASTD HQ
- ASTD chapters
- *Chief Learning Officer* magazine subscribers
- CSTD—Canadian Society for Training and Development (formerly OSTD)
- ICF—International Coach Federation
- IFTDO—International Federation of Training and Development Organisations
- ISA—Instructional Systems Association
- ISPI—International Society for Performance Improvement
- NVO2—Dutch training and development association
- ODN—Organization Development Network.

3. Sample Size

The final sample size included 2,128 responses, representing 5.9 percent of the targeted population.

Demographics from this sample are similar to the demographics of ASTD's actual membership. The margin of error for conclusions is +/–2.9 percent. This means that if the survey were to be conducted again, there is an extremely high probability that the results would be exactly the same. The margin of error for this study is in line with commonly accepted standards for survey research. Demographics of the survey respondents can be found in appendix D.

Phase IV: Final Refinement and Confirmation

1. Project Team Refinement

Using information collected from the survey results, DDI and Rothwell & Associates Inc. created a final model for approval by the ASTD project team and advisory committee. It included slight modifications made in response to a content analysis of written comments from survey respondents. Each written comment was evaluated in terms of its relationship to the model and how frequently it was mentioned. Changes were reviewed in a group setting and approved by subject matter experts when appropriate. Usually, any revisions represented clear omissions from the model. These revisions included clarifying words for particular key actions or key knowledge areas. All these revisions are reflected in the final ASTD Competency Model in appendix A. Copies of the final revisions are on file at ASTD.

2. Project Team/Advisory Committee Approval

A meeting was held with the ASTD project team and advisory committee to review the final competency model structure, gather feedback, and suggest revisions. Minor revisions were made to the model graphic. After the model was finalized, the project team began to draft the structure and content of this report. The end product represents the systematic development and phased process for creating a well constructed and validated WLP competency model.

Demographics and Summary of Survey Responses

Demographic Analysis[1]

Job or role analysis is most accurate when the sample providing the ratings is representative of the targeted population. This study relied on a broad sampling of WLP-related professional organizations to define the target population. Participating professional organizations included groups such as ASTD members, *Chief Learning Officer* magazine subscribers, International Federation of Training and Development Organisations, and the International Society for Performance Improvement (see Phase III of the Research Methodology section in appendix C). In this study respondents' demographics indicate that a broad range of groups has been represented. It is not unusual for differences in ratings to appear based on demographic characteristics. Entire bodies of research outline differences in perceptions based on race, gender, age, and national origin. In this study we checked to make sure that there were no unusually large differences in groups that might affect the use of the competencies and AOEs.

Competency Analysis

Differences in competency ratings based on demographics were evaluated using two criteria:

1. **Absolute importance rating**—All competencies were rated using 5-point importance scales. When average importance ratings reached a minimum rating criteria of 3.0, we considered the competency to be valid and important for the WLP model. We examined each demographic grouping to ensure that all groups rated competencies at or above this minimum rating.

2. **Size of differences**—Cohen's *d* statistic[2] is a commonly used measure of the size of differences between groups. Although there are no commonly accepted criteria for determining if a given *d* statistic is large enough to be important, Cohen recommended that a *d* of .25 is a small effect, .50 is a medium-size effect, and .75 is a large effect. All demographic groups were compared to determine effect sizes.

Demographic	All Ratings Above 3.0?	Average Effect Size
Gender	Yes	.17
Age	Yes	.10*
Race (Caucasian vs. Other)	Yes	.20
National Origin	Yes	.01

*Average effect size across all possible comparisons.

Conclusion. Overall, few differences exist between demographic groups. All groups find the competencies to be important for their current jobs. Effect sizes show that females and non-Caucasians tend to rate some competencies as somewhat more important than do males and Caucasians, respectively. Although differences do appear, they are small and have little impact on the conclusions drawn in this study.

Area of Expertise Analysis

Typically, WLP professionals demonstrate expertise in only four or five of the AOEs. Therefore, we would not expect raters to provide high importance ratings for all AOEs (see criterion 1 under Competency Analysis above). For AOEs, we focused on group differences (that is, Cohen's *d*) rather than absolute ratings of importance. All demographic groups were compared to determine effect sizes.

Demographic	Average Effect Size
Gender	.04
Age	.05*
Race (Caucasian vs. Other)	.12
National Origin	.01

*Average effect size across all possible comparisons.

Conclusion. Overall, very few differences exist between demographic groups. Effect sizes show that differences between demographic groupings are almost nonexistent and have virtually no impact on the conclusions drawn in this study.

---

[1] Further information about the demographic comparisons made in this report can be obtained by contacting ASTD.

[2] Cohen, J. (1962). The statistical power of abnormal-social psychological research: A review. *Journal of Abnormal and Social Psychology*, 65, 145–153.

Demographics

The following pages contain the demographics of the 2,128 respondents to the competency survey.

Years of experience in the workplace learning and performance profession:

	%*
Less than 1 year	1.1
1–2 years	4.5
3–5 years	16.5
6–10 years	24.8
11–15 years	17.5
More than 15 years	35.6

* If the percentages total slightly more or less than 100 in this or any of the following columns, it is because the figures have been rounded.

Please indicate your span of control in your organization. (Use the labels below as descriptive headings, not actual job titles.)

	%
Executive—oversee multiple functional areas (for example, CEO, CLO, Vice President)	6.5
Director—oversee an entire functional area	18.3
Manager—oversee department within a functional area	23.5
Supervisor—manage a group within a department	5.5
Team leader—manage a work group or team	6.5
Individual contributor—member of a team or independent employee	24.9
Independent consultant	9.5
University professor or college instructor	1.4
Full-time student	0.4
Unemployed	0.4
Other (please specify)	3.2

Primary Area of Job Responsibility (please identify which *one* of the following *best* describes your major area of responsibility):

	%
Training	38.9
Instructional Design	10.9
Career Development	1.4
Coaching	1.5
Leadership Development, Management Development, Executive Development	11.5
Performance Consulting	7.2
Change Management, Organization Development, Organizational Effectiveness	10.7
Knowledge Management	2.0
Measurement and Evaluation	1.9
Human Resource Management	4.9
Other specific human resource area (for example, staffing, selection, compensation, employee relations, etc.)	0.6
Other (please specify)	8.4

Years of experience in the Primary Area of Job Responsibility identified in the previous question:

	%
Less than 1 year	2.6
1–2 years	8.5
3–5 years	26.2
6–10 years	26.4
11–15 years	15.6
More than 15 years	20.8

Please indicate any current certificates or certifications that you currently hold that are relevant for this profession. (Select all that apply.)

	%
Association or association-affiliated certificate/certification	32.0
Vendor certificate/certification	34.6
College or university certificate/certification	65.2
Other certificate/certification	16.7

Which of the following best describes your organization?

	%
For-profit organization	50.6
Nonprofit (not including government, academic, or military)	13.7
Academic institution	6.3
Government agency	7.6
Military branch or service	0.4
Consulting firm	11.3
Independent consultant or sole proprietor	5.5
Other (please specify)	4.5

Industry (please select *one* industry classification that *best* describes where you conduct most of your work):

	%
Agriculture, Forestry, Fishing and Hunting	0.5
Arts, Entertainment and Recreation (including Lodging/Hospitality)	1.6
Broadcasting and Communications	1.9
Business Schools and Computer Management Training	0.8
Colleges, Universities, and Professional Schools	6.1
Finance and Insurance	15.9
Health Care and Social Assistance	12.2
Information (other services)	3.2
Management Consulting Services (including HRD consulting)	10.2
Manufacturing	12.1
National Security	1.2
Public Administration (including government)	6.3
Real Estate and Rental and Leading	0.5
Retail Trade	3.6
Software Publishing	1.5
Transportation and Warehousing	1.6
Utilities	3.1
Wholesale Trade	1.0
Other (please specify)	16.7

Work location (please indicate the region in which you currently work):

	%
Africa	0.5
Asia	1.6
Australia	2.1
Canada	1.2
Europe	3.5
Central America	0.1
South America	0.6
United States	87.4
Other country	3.0

Please indicate all the association memberships/affiliations you currently hold:

	%
AITD—Australian Institute of Training and Development	3.5
AOM—Academy of Management	1.0
ASTD HQ	81.2
ASTD chapter	41.7
CIPD—Chartered Institute of Personnel and Development (U.K. and Ireland)	0.5
CLO magazine subscriber	6.3
CPD—Continuing Personal/Professional Development (U.K.)	0.4
CSTD—Canadian Society for Training and Development (formerly OSTD)	1.0
ICF—International Coach Federation	1.2
IFTDO—International Federation of Training and Development Organisations	0.7
ISA—Instructional Systems Association	0.1
ISPI—International Society for Performance Improvement	15.6
NVO2—Dutch training and development association	4.4
ODN—Organization Development Network	6.7
SIOP—Society for Industrial and Organizational Psychology	1.1

Educational background (please indicate the *highest level* of education you have achieved):

	%
High school diploma/certificate or equivalent (that is, prior to university)	1.2
Some trade/business school training (may include special degrees or certifications)	1.3
Two-year degree (for example, trade or business school certificate/degree, associate of arts degree)	1.9
Some university/college education	7.8
University/College graduate (for example, bachelor of arts, bachelor of science)	19.8
Some post-graduate education	14.3
Master's degree (for example, master of arts, master of sciences, master of business administration)	44.0
Advanced graduate or professional degree (for example, doctor of philosophy, doctor of medicine)	9.6
None of the above	0.0

Age:

	%
29 or less	5.4
30 to 39	24.6
40 to 49	34.7
50 to 59	31.5
60 or over	3.8

Gender:

	%
Female	66.9
Male	33.1

Race or ethnic group (United States only):

	%
Black (African American)	4.5
American Indian Eskimo or Aleut	0.6
Asian	1.8
White (Caucasian)	87.4
Hispanic	2.6
Mixed Race	1.9
Other (please specify)	1.2

ASTD is interested in your reactions on whether or not to rename the profession. Please indicate which name or label you prefer our profession to be called:

	%
Training	1.4
Training and Development	30.9
Human Resource Development	14.2
Workplace Learning and Performance	32.0
Workforce Development	10.7
Other (please specify)	10.9

Future of the Profession: ASTD Conference 5/19/03

Number of respondents: 63

The data in this section was obtained during the *Future of the Profession* session conducted during ASTD's 2003 International Conference and Exposition.

Current Level:

	%
Executive—Vice President or higher, or officer of the company	39.3
Manager—Manages large projects or large permanent groups	21.3
Supervisor—Manages a department or group	9.8
Entry—Manages self or occasional small groups or teams	8.2
Private Consultant—Works independently or is self-employed	21.3

Years in Workplace Learning and Performance Profession:

	%
Less than 1 year	1.6
1–2 years	4.8
3–5 years	12.7
6–10 years	12.7
11–15 years	23.8
More than 15 years	44.4

Area of Professional Expertise (Multiple selections represented):

	%
Training	46.0
Organizational Development	22.2
Management Development	19.0
Human Resource Management	6.3
Other (please specify)	23.8

Years of Experience in This Area of Professional Expertise:

	%
Less than 1 year	0.0
1–2 years	4.8
3–5 years	17.5
6–10 years	14.3
11–15 years	22.2
More than 15 years	41.3

Educational Background:

	%
High school diploma or equivalent (GED)	0.0
Some trade/business school training	1.6
Two-year degree (for example, a trade or business school certificate/degree, associate degree)	1.6
Some college	3.2
College graduate (for example, B.A., B.S.)	20.6
Some graduate school	12.7
Master's degree (for example, M.A., M.S., M.B.A.)	44.4
Advanced graduate or professional degree (for example, Ph.D., J.D.)	15.9

Industry:

	%
Agriculture/Mining/Construction	2.1
Trade	2.1
Government	8.5
Finance, Insurance, Real Estate	10.6
Durables	12.8
Non-Durables	0.0
Information Technology	19.1
Health Care	2.1
Services	38.3
Transportation/Public Utilities	4.3

Number of Publications in Profession:

	%
None	41.8
1–5	32.7
6–10	5.5
11–20	5.5
21–30	5.5
31 or more	9.1

Number of Times You Have Presented at Professional Conferences:

	%
None	25.9
1–5	39.7
6–10	1.7
11–20	8.6
21–30	8.6
31 or more	15.5

Age:

	%
29 or less	0.0
30 to 39	27.1
40 to 49	23.7
50 to 59	40.7
60 or over	8.5

Gender:

	%
Female	61.0
Male	39.0

Location:

	%
Non-U.S. (please specify)	8.5
United States	91.5

U.S. Respondents Only: Race or Ethnic Group:

	%
African American	1.9
Asian American	1.9
Caucasian	92.5
Hispanic	3.8
American Indian, Eskimo, or Aleut	0.0
Mixed Race	0.0
Other (please specify)	0.0

Would you be interested in further participation in this hallmark study?

	%
Yes	61.9
No	38.1

ASTD Thought Leader Interviews

Demographic Information

The data in this section was obtained primarily through interviews with thought leaders conducted during ASTD's 2003 International Conference and Exposition. Some additional interviews were conducted by phone.

Current Level:
(Please identify which one of the following *best* describes your current level):
Number of Respondents: 48

	%
Executive—Vice President or higher, or officer of the company	54.2
Manager—Manages large projects or large permanent groups	22.9
Supervisor—Manages a department or group	0.0
Entry—Manages self or occasional small groups or teams	0.0
Private Consultant—Works independently or is self-employed	16.7
Other	6.2

Years in Workplace Learning and Performance Profession:
Number of Respondents: 48

	%
Less than 1 year	0.0
1–2 years	0.0
3–5 years	8.3
6–10 years	6.2
11–15 years	16.7
More than 15 years	68.8

Area of Professional Expertise
(Please identify which one of the following *best* describes your area of expertise):
Number of Respondents: 47

	%
Training	27.7
Organizational Development	6.4
Management Development	10.6
Human Resource Management	6.4
Other	48.9

Years of Experience in This Area of Professional Expertise:
Number of Respondents: 47

	%
Less than 1 year	0.0
1–2 years	2.1
3–5 years	4.3
6–10 years	6.4
11–15 years	17.0
More than 15 years	70.2

Educational Background (Please indicate the *highest* level of education you have achieved):
Number of Respondents: 47

	%
High school diploma or equivalent (GED)	0.0
Some trade/business school training	0.0
Two-year degree (for example, a trade or business school certificate/degree, associate's degree)	0.0
Some college	0.0
College graduate (for example, B.A., B.S.)	8.5
Some graduate school	4.3
Master's degree (for example, M.A., M.S., M.B.A.)	48.9
Advanced graduate or professional degree (for example, Ph.D., J.D.)	38.3

Industry (Please select *one* industry classification that *best* describes where you conduct most of your work):
Number of Respondents: 47

	%
Agriculture/Mining/Construction	0.0
Trade	0.0
Government	4.3
Finance, Insurance, Real Estate	4.3
Durables	0.0
Non-Durables	0.0
Information Technology	10.6
Health Care	2.1
Services	25.5
Transportation/Public Utilities	2.1
Other	51.1

Number of Publications in Profession (Include published white papers, articles, or books):
Number of Respondents: 45

	%
None	22.2
1 to 5	8.9
6 to 10	17.8
11 to 20	15.6
21 to 30	8.9
31 or more	26.7

Number of Times You Have Presented at Professional Conferences:
Number of Respondents: 47

	%
None	6.4
1 to 5	10.6
6 to 10	4.3
11 to 20	27.7
21 to 30	8.5
31 or more	42.6

Age:
Number of Respondents: 47

	%
29 or less	0.0
30 to 39	14.9
40 to 49	29.8
50 to 59	44.7
60 or over	10.6

Gender:
Number of Respondents: 48

	%
Female	43.8
Male	56.3

Location (Please indicate in which country you currently work):
Number of Respondents: 48

	%
United States	79.2
Non-U.S.	20.8

U.S. Respondents Only: Race or Ethnic Group:
Number of Respondents: 38

	%
African American	2.6
Asian American	0.0
Caucasian	94.7
Hispanic	2.6
American Indian, Eskimo, or Aleut	0.0
Mixed Race	0.0
Other (please specify)	0.0

Research Summary

The following pages contain the importance ratings obtained from the 2,128 respondents to the competency survey. In most cases, ratings were made using a 5-point scale. The percentage of responses is given in the first five columns, and the average score is given in the last column. To calculate averages, analysts assigned a number to each label on the scale (for example, Unnecessary = 1, Slightly Important = 2, etc.). For importance ratings, any average score was considered to be meaningful when it equaled or exceeded 3.0.

How important is the role for effective performance in your current job?

	Unnecessary	Slightly Important	Moderately Important	Very Important	Essential	Average
Learning Strategist	1.9	7.0	15.7	38.7	36.7	4.01
Business Partner	3.2	7.9	16.1	33.3	39.5	3.98
Project Manager	1.4	5.5	15.9	38.2	39.0	4.08
Professional Specialist	1.4	4.1	14.2	34.6	45.7	4.19

Please indicate the percentage of time you spend performing each of the roles in your current job. (Your total must equal 100 points.)

	%
Learning Strategist	21.8
Business Partner	20.0
Project Manager	23.2
Professional Specialist	27.9
Other role	7.1

How important is each key action for effective performance in your current job?

ANALYZING NEEDS AND PROPOSING SOLUTIONS	Unnecessary	Slightly Important	Moderately Important	Very Important	Essential	Average
Gathers information about client needs	0.9	4.0	11.7	35.0	48.4	4.26
Diagnoses learning and performance issues	3.1	12.9	24.5	35.0	24.5	3.65
Generates multiple alternatives	1.2	7.9	25.1	43.9	21.9	3.77
Searches for innovative solutions	1.2	6.0	21.6	45.3	25.9	3.89
Chooses appropriate solution(s)	1.4	3.8	14.9	42.1	37.8	4.11
Recognizes impact	1.5	5.1	17.8	43.0	32.6	4.00
Proposes solution(s)	0.8	2.5	12.6	44.2	40.0	4.20
OVERALL	0.5	2.1	10.9	42.7	43.8	4.27

How important is each key action for effective performance in your current job?

APPLYING BUSINESS ACUMEN	Unnecessary	Slightly Important	Moderately Important	Very Important	Essential	Average
Understands the business	0.9	5.1	17.1	38.6	38.3	4.08
Understands business operations	0.6	3.9	17.8	43.2	34.5	4.07
Applies financial data	6.0	20.2	36.7	27.2	9.9	3.15
Uses business terminology to gain credibility	2.4	7.6	23.5	40.8	25.7	3.80
Recognizes business priorities	1.9	5.5	14.9	42.2	35.5	4.04
Creates a value proposition	2.7	7.2	19.1	38.3	32.8	3.91
Advances the learning and performance business agenda	1.7	5.4	17.8	42.0	33.1	4.00
OVERALL	0.6	4.2	19.2	47.9	28.1	3.99

How important is each key action for effective performance in your current job?

DRIVING RESULTS	Unnecessary	Slightly Important	Moderately Important	Very Important	Essential	Average
Targets improvement opportunities	2.3	7.6	24.9	42.8	22.3	3.75
Establishes goals and objectives	1.7	7.4	19.3	39.5	32.1	3.93
Orchestrates effort to achieve results	1.5	6.8	21.1	42.9	27.7	3.89
Overcomes obstacles	1.2	4.2	18.1	42.8	33.7	4.04
Provides courageous leadership	2.3	6.3	18.7	37.6	35.0	3.97
OVERALL	1.0	5.7	20.0	45.1	28.2	3.94

How important is each key action for effective performance in your current job?

PLANNING & IMPLEMENTING ASSIGNMENTS	Unnecessary	Slightly Important	Moderately Important	Very Important	Essential	Average
Establishes parameters and forecasts outcomes	3.0	9.4	28.5	42.2	16.9	3.61
Uses planning tools to create project plans	6.6	21.4	32.1	27.8	12.1	3.18
Manages budget	9.0	14.4	24.9	29.2	22.5	3.42
Determines tasks and resources	2.7	9.7	22.5	40.3	24.9	3.75
Plans for contingencies	2.0	10.0	25.8	40.4	21.7	3.70
Mobilizes resources	1.3	6.0	17.2	44.3	31.1	3.98
Manages time	0.6	3.9	12.2	41.6	41.7	4.20
Tracks progress and ensures completion	1.0	3.6	11.2	42.0	42.1	4.21
OVERALL	0.5	5.6	19.4	48.3	26.2	3.94

How important is each key action for effective performance in your current job?

THINKING STRATEGICALLY	Unnecessary	Slightly Important	Moderately Important	Very Important	Essential	Average
Understands external factors impacting learning and performance	2.4	10.3	25.0	36.4	25.9	3.73
Understands the organizational context for learning and performance	1.5	4.4	15.0	40.1	39.0	4.11
Recognizes and acts on emerging opportunities	1.8	8.0	26.1	40.7	23.5	3.76
Builds strategic alignment	2.8	8.3	18.3	36.6	34.1	3.91
Develops learning and performance strategies	2.3	6.0	16.7	42.4	32.6	3.97
Operates from a systems perspective	2.3	5.6	17.4	35.6	39.2	4.04
OVERALL	1.2	5.1	19.5	44.3	30.0	3.97

How important is each key action for effective performance in your current job?

BUILDING TRUST	Unnecessary	Slightly Important	Moderately Important	Very Important	Essential	Average
Operates with integrity	0.2	0.2	1.7	15.8	82.1	4.79
Discloses position	0.6	2.1	12.5	39.7	45.2	4.27
Maintains confidentiality	0.1	0.8	2.5	15.6	81.0	4.77
Leads by example	0.3	0.6	3.3	23.6	72.1	4.67
Treats people fairly	0.2	0.3	2.5	20.2	76.8	4.73
Ensures compliance with legal, ethical, and regulatory requirements	1.1	1.3	5.2	18.4	74.0	4.63
OVERALL	0.2	0.5	2.7	20.9	75.7	4.71

How important is each key action for effective performance in your current job?

COMMUNICATING EFFECTIVELY	Unnecessary	Slightly Important	Moderately Important	Very Important	Essential	Average
Develops and deploys effective communication strategies	0.6	2.1	10.9	40.4	46.1	4.29
Delivers clear messages	0.1	0.3	2.3	32.2	65.0	4.62
Presents with impact	0.3	0.8	8.1	36.7	54.0	4.43
Adjusts message content and delivery	0.2	1.0	6.7	38.0	54.2	4.45
Demonstrates active listening	0.2	0.8	2.6	30.5	65.8	4.61
Invites dialogue	0.2	0.6	4.8	33.0	61.4	4.55
Creates clear written communication	0.2	0.4	4.6	36.0	58.7	4.53
Masters multiple communication methods	0.2	1.4	10.1	35.0	53.3	4.40
OVERALL	0.1	0.3	2.8	36.4	60.4	4.57

How important is each key action for effective performance in your current job?

INFLUENCING STAKEHOLDERS	Unnecessary	Slightly Important	Moderately Important	Very Important	Essential	Average
Analyzes stakeholder perspectives	2.9	6.0	17.9	42.3	31.0	3.92
Establishes a marketing strategy	5.2	11.0	27.4	39.3	17.0	3.52
Communicates a strong value proposition	2.6	5.9	18.5	40.7	32.2	3.94
Builds energy and support	1.8	4.8	14.8	43.3	35.3	4.06
Gains commitment to the solution	1.8	4.5	14.5	39.0	40.2	4.11
OVERALL	1.5	5.5	19.7	45.5	27.8	3.93

How important is each key action for effective performance in your current job?

LEVERAGING DIVERSITY	Unnecessary	Slightly Important	Moderately Important	Very Important	Essential	Average
Conveys respect for different perspectives	0.7	2.1	11.0	45.4	40.8	4.24
Expands own awareness	1.4	5.0	18.0	41.0	34.6	4.02
Adapts behavior to accommodate others	0.5	2.4	15.4	44.8	37.0	4.16
Champions diversity	3.2	7.9	20.2	35.8	32.9	3.87
Leverages diverse contributions	1.6	5.6	21.2	41.7	29.9	3.93
Accommodates global differences	8.2	12.6	21.9	32.3	25.1	3.54
OVERALL	0.9	6.2	23.9	44.5	24.4	3.85

How important is each key action for effective performance in your current job?

NETWORKING AND PARTNERING	Unnecessary	Slightly Important	Moderately Important	Very Important	Essential	Average
Networks with others	0.4	2.5	15.2	42.4	39.5	4.18
Benchmarks and shares best practices	0.7	5.5	23.8	44.3	25.6	3.89
Establishes common goals	1.1	3.4	21.5	44.7	29.3	3.98
Develops partnering relationships	0.5	3.0	13.8	43.6	39.0	4.18
Generates new collaborative possibilities	0.7	3.6	19.3	46.5	29.8	4.01
OVERALL	0.5	2.6	20.8	48.0	28.1	4.01

How important is each key action for effective performance in your current job?

DEMONSTRATING ADAPTABILITY	Unnecessary	Slightly Important	Moderately Important	Very Important	Essential	Average
Seeks to understand changes	0.6	1.4	10.9	46.9	40.2	4.25
Approaches change positively	0.2	0.8	5.0	38.0	56.0	4.49
Remains open to different ideas and approaches	0.1	1.0	5.3	45.8	47.8	4.40
Adjusts behavior	0.3	0.9	6.8	42.4	49.7	4.40
Adapts to handle implementation challenges	0.5	1.9	9.6	44.3	43.6	4.29
OVERALL	0.3	0.7	7.5	46.0	45.5	4.36

How important is each key action for effective performance in your current job?

MODELING PERSONAL DEVELOPMENT	Unnecessary	Slightly Important	Moderately Important	Very Important	Essential	Average
Models self-mastery in learning	0.3	2.6	15.5	43.9	37.7	4.16
Seeks learning activities	0.2	2.2	12.4	44.9	40.4	4.23
Takes risks in learning	0.9	5.8	24.4	40.0	29.0	3.90
Maximizes learning opportunities	0.3	2.3	15.1	41.8	40.5	4.20
Applies new knowledge or skill	0.1	1.7	10.5	42.2	45.4	4.31
Maintains professional knowledge	0.1	1.7	6.5	33.8	57.8	4.48
OVERALL	0.3	1.5	14.2	45.3	38.8	4.21

Please consider all the competencies you have just rated. Select the *top three* you believe will be the *most important* for the effective performance of your job in the next three years. Please select exactly three competencies.

	Response Total
Analyzing Needs and Proposing Solutions	51%
Applying Business Acumen	19%
Driving Results	30%
Planning and Implementing Assignments	19%
Thinking Strategically	41%
Building Trust	25%
Communicating Effectively	40%
Influencing Stakeholders	22%
Leveraging Diversity	5%
Networking and Partnering	18%
Demonstrating Adaptability	20%
Modeling Personal Development	10%

WHERE YOU SPEND YOUR TIME
Please indicate the percentage of time you spent performing each of the professional areas of expertise in your job during the past year. Your total should equal 100 percent.

	%
Career Planning and Talent Management	6.1
Coaching	10.6
Delivering Training	17.3
Designing Learning	18.5
Facilitating Organizational Change	9.0
Improving Human Performance	8.8
Managing Organizational Knowledge	6.1
Managing the Learning Function	11.3
Measuring and Evaluating	7.6
Other Professional/Technical Role	5.0

IMPORTANCE
Overall, how important is each professional area of expertise for effective performance in your current job?

	Unnecessary	Slightly Important	Moderately Important	Very Important	Essential	Average
Career Planning and Talent Management	11.1	24.6	28.2	25.4	10.7	3.00
Coaching	3.6	14.5	24.4	32.8	24.6	3.60
Delivering Training	5.6	12.0	18.8	26.6	37.0	3.77
Designing Learning	2.9	7.8	16.7	29.4	43.1	4.02
Facilitating Organizational Change	5.6	13.0	21.8	32.6	27.0	3.63
Improving Human Performance	3.3	9.3	17.8	38.1	31.4	3.85
Managing Organizational Knowledge	6.5	17.3	30.3	31.3	14.6	3.30
Managing the Learning Function	7.4	13.3	20.9	29.1	29.2	3.59
Measuring and Evaluating	2.6	10.6	24.6	38.3	23.9	3.70

Which of the following professional areas of expertise is most likely to become more important for effective performance in your job in the next three years? (You may select only one.)

	Response Total
Career Planning and Talent Management	7.6%
Coaching	7.0%
Delivering Training	5.1%
Designing Learning	8.0%
Facilitating Organizational Change	19.9%
Improving Human Performance	20.1%
Managing Organizational Knowledge	10.3%
Managing the Learning Function	7.6%
Measuring and Evaluating	12.5%
Other (please specify)	1.6%

From the following list, please select one area in which you have the most expertise:

	Number of Raters
Career Planning and Talent Management	100
Coaching	187
Delivering Training	530
Designing Learning	442
Facilitating Organizational Change	220
Improving Human Performance	216
Managing Organizational Knowledge	79
Managing the Learning Function	239
Measuring and Evaluating	106
I do not have expertise in any of these areas	49

Note: Survey respondents were allowed to rate as many areas of expertise as they wanted.

Key Knowledge Areas: How important is each key knowledge area for effective performance in this professional area of expertise?

CAREER PLANNING AND TALENT MANAGEMENT	Unnecessary	Slightly Important	Moderately Important	Very Important	Essential	Average
Workforce planning approaches	1.0	5.0	19.0	49.0	26.0	3.94
Succession and replacement-planning approaches	0.0	4.0	10.0	41.0	45.0	4.27
Job analysis tools and procedures	0.0	6.0	23.0	43.0	28.0	3.93
Career development theories and approaches	0.0	8.2	22.4	37.8	31.6	3.93
Individual and organizational assessment tools, including assessment center methodologies	0.0	2.0	14.1	52.5	31.3	4.13
Ethical standards and legal issues in career counseling and organizational restructuring	0.0	7.0	15.0	34.0	44.0	4.15
Career counseling approaches	1.0	8.0	25.0	36.0	30.0	3.86
Coaching approaches	0.0	1.0	17.0	45.0	37.0	4.18
Performance consulting approaches	0.0	2.0	14.0	49.0	35.0	4.17
Managerial and leadership development best practices	0.0	1.0	9.0	39.0	51.0	4.40
Performance management systems and techniques	0.0	3.1	17.5	46.4	33.0	4.09
Approaches to maximize workplace diversity	2.0	9.0	28.0	43.0	18.0	3.66
Resources for career exploration and lifelong learning	2.0	5.1	19.2	42.4	31.3	3.96

Key Actions: How important is each key action for effective performance in this professional area of expertise?

CAREER PLANNING AND TALENT MANAGEMENT	Unnecessary	Slightly Important	Moderately Important	Very Important	Essential	Average
Creates success profiles	1.0	6.1	14.1	45.5	33.3	4.04
Identifies capability requirements	1.0	3.0	8.1	45.5	42.4	4.25
Coordinates succession planning	1.0	5.1	17.2	37.4	39.4	4.09
Implements individual and organizational assessments	0.0	2.0	11.2	45.9	40.8	4.26
Facilitates the career development planning process	0.0	5.1	12.1	36.4	46.5	4.24
Organizes delivery of developmental resources	0.0	3.0	17.2	39.4	40.4	4.17
Initiates strategic development programs	1.0	3.0	20.2	39.4	36.4	4.07
Equips managers to develop their people	2.0	4.1	9.2	28.6	56.1	4.33
Promotes high-performance workplaces	0.0	3.1	12.2	38.8	45.9	4.28
Administers performance management systems	2.0	4.1	24.5	42.9	26.5	3.88
Conducts career counseling sessions	3.0	10.1	26.3	28.3	32.3	3.77
Facilitates career transitions	3.1	11.2	23.5	32.7	29.6	3.74

Key Knowledge Areas: How important is each key knowledge area for effective performance in this professional area of expertise?

COACHING	Unnecessary	Slightly Important	Moderately Important	Very Important	Essential	Average
Standards of conduct	0.0	1.6	9.1	37.4	51.9	4.40
Ethical guidelines	0.5	1.1	4.3	33.7	60.4	4.52
Core coaching competencies (setting the foundation, co-creating the relationship, communicating effectively, facilitating learning and results)	0.0	0.0	2.7	25.5	71.7	4.69

Key Actions: How important is each key action for effective performance in this professional area of expertise?

COACHING	Unnecessary	Slightly Important	Moderately Important	Very Important	Essential	Average
Meets ethical guidelines and professional standards	0.0	0.5	6.5	31.4	61.6	4.54
Establishes coaching agreement	0.5	1.6	8.6	35.5	53.8	4.40
Establishes trust and intimacy with the client	0.0	0.0	1.6	16.1	82.3	4.81
Displays coaching presence	0.0	0.0	7.5	36.0	56.5	4.49
Demonstrates active listening	0.0	0.5	1.1	22.2	76.2	4.74
Asks powerful questions	0.0	0.5	5.4	34.9	59.1	4.53
Uses direct communication	0.0	0.0	5.9	37.1	57.0	4.51
Creates awareness	0.0	1.1	8.1	41.1	49.7	4.39
Designs actions	0.0	2.2	8.6	45.2	44.1	4.31
Develops goals and plans	0.0	2.2	4.3	41.6	51.9	4.43
Manages progress and accountability	0.5	0.5	5.4	35.9	57.6	4.49

Key Knowledge Areas: How important is each key knowledge area for effective performance in this professional area of expertise?

DELIVERING TRAINING	Unnecessary	Slightly Important	Moderately Important	Very Important	Essential	Average
Adult learning theories and techniques	0.2	1.3	8.9	34.0	55.7	4.44
Instructional design theory and methods	0.6	3.8	19.0	40.6	36.1	4.08
Various delivery options/media, such as online learning, classroom training, print media, etc.	0.2	2.5	13.7	41.2	42.4	4.23
Existing learning technologies and support systems, such as collaborative learning software, learning management systems, and authoring tools	2.7	14.2	30.7	36.8	15.6	3.48
Emerging learning technologies and support systems	2.1	11.9	35.5	37.6	12.9	3.47
Presentation techniques and tools	0.0	0.6	6.8	35.3	57.3	4.49
Organizational work environment and systems, including learning delivery channels	1.3	6.7	28.5	43.9	19.6	3.74
Individual learning styles, such as audiovisual	0.0	2.1	14.0	37.1	46.9	4.29
Cultural differences in learning styles, communication, classroom behavior, etc.	0.2	4.4	16.6	39.0	39.8	4.14
Own personal learning preferences, such as a preference for lecture or experience-based learning and how that impacts delivery capabilities	0.8	7.0	25.4	38.9	27.9	3.86
Tools for determining learning preferences such as a preference for lecture or experience-based learning, etc.	0.8	8.4	24.8	43.8	22.3	3.78
Familiarity with content being taught and how the solution addresses the need (that is, context)	0.4	0.8	8.1	30.7	60.0	4.49
Legal and ethical issues relevant for delivering training	0.9	7.8	21.2	36.6	33.5	3.94

Key Actions: How important is each key action for effective performance in this professional area of expertise?

DELIVERING TRAINING	Unnecessary	Slightly Important	Moderately Important	Very Important	Essential	Average
Prepares for training delivery	0.0	0.6	4.0	23.8	71.6	4.66
Aligns learning solutions with course objectives and learner needs	0.0	0.2	4.2	32.6	63.0	4.58
Conveys objectives	0.0	0.8	4.6	36.3	58.3	4.52
Delivers various learning methodologies	0.0	0.6	9.0	40.0	50.4	4.40
Facilitates learning	0.0	0.2	1.7	26.5	71.6	4.69
Encourages participation and builds learner motivation	0.0	0.0	2.7	23.6	73.8	4.71
Establishes credibility as instructor	0.0	0.6	1.1	26.5	71.8	4.69
Manages the learning environment	0.4	1.0	9.8	42.0	46.8	4.34
Delivers constructive feedback	0.0	1.3	10.2	43.1	45.4	4.33
Creates a positive learning climate	0.0	0.4	2.3	27.2	70.2	4.67
Ensures learning outcomes	0.0	1.3	7.5	39.7	51.5	4.41
Evaluates solutions	0.0	2.1	11.2	48.9	37.7	4.22

Key Knowledge Areas: How important is each key knowledge area for effective performance in this professional area of expertise?

DESIGNING LEARNING	Unnecessary	Slightly Important	Moderately Important	Very Important	Essential	Average
Adult learning theory	0.5	2.0	9.7	31.7	56.1	4.41
Instructional design theory and process	0.2	2.1	8.9	33.0	55.8	4.42
Various instructional methods, such as lecture, discussion, practical exercise, feedback, etc.	0.0	1.4	6.1	34.3	58.2	4.49
Various delivery options/media, such as online learning, classroom training, print media, etc.	0.0	1.6	10.1	39.7	48.6	4.35
Job/Task analysis and competency modeling	0.7	4.6	20.3	42.5	32.0	4.00
Content knowledge or techniques to elicit content from subject matter experts	0.5	2.3	12.0	39.6	45.6	4.28
Assessment methods and formats, such as multiple choice, hands-on, open-ended response, etc.	0.2	6.0	18.0	44.0	31.8	4.01
Learning technologies and support systems, such as collaborative learning, software, learning management systems, and authoring tools	1.4	13.3	27.0	36.8	21.5	3.64
New and emerging learning technologies and support systems	1.4	11.7	29.4	36.9	20.6	3.64
Business strategy, drivers, or needs associated with possible learning interventions	1.4	5.7	24.1	40.0	28.7	3.89
Research methods, including information scanning, data gathering, and analysis	1.4	10.8	28.4	39.4	20.1	3.66
Individual, group, and organizational differences that influence learning, such as cultural norms/values, cognitive abilities, learning preferences, previous experience, and motivation	1.1	5.5	18.6	42.7	32.1	3.99
Legal and ethical issues related to designing learning, including accessibility and intellectual property	1.8	9.2	26.6	39.2	23.2	3.73
Differences between e-learning and traditional courses and their implications	2.1	7.6	25.1	35.6	29.7	3.83

Key Actions: How important is each key action for effective performance in this professional area of expertise?

DESIGNING LEARNING	Unnecessary	Slightly Important	Moderately Important	Very Important	Essential	Average
Applies adult learning theory	0.5	3.0	7.3	33.7	55.5	4.41
Collaborates with others	0.5	1.8	8.1	39.2	50.5	4.37
Conducts a needs assessment	1.4	2.1	10.6	34.3	51.6	4.33
Designs a curriculum or program	0.2	1.4	5.3	38.5	54.6	4.46
Designs instructional material	0.2	0.9	4.8	32.6	61.4	4.54
Analyzes and selects technologies	1.2	3.9	17.5	47.5	30.0	4.01
Integrates technology options	1.2	5.5	23.7	45.2	24.4	3.86
Develops instructional materials	0.2	1.6	5.8	31.6	60.8	4.51
Evaluates learning design	1.4	1.2	11.8	38.6	47.1	4.29
Manages others	4.6	11.3	27.1	35.4	21.6	3.58
Manages and implements projects	3.0	4.8	18.4	40.1	33.6	3.97

Key Knowledge Areas: How important is each key knowledge area for effective performance in this professional area of expertise?

FACILITATING ORGANIZATIONAL CHANGE	Unnecessary	Slightly Important	Moderately Important	Very Important	Essential	Average
Systems thinking and open systems theory, such as the organization is an open system influenced by the external environment	0.9	3.2	13.6	31.4	50.9	4.28
Chaos and complexity theory	5.5	13.7	37.0	31.1	12.8	3.32
Appreciative inquiry theory (a theory of organizing and method for changing social systems—one of the more significant innovations in action research in the past decade)	4.1	11.1	26.7	38.7	19.4	3.58
Action research theory	2.8	12.0	32.9	35.2	17.1	3.52
Organizational systems and cultures, including political dynamics in organizational setting	0.0	1.9	7.1	34.4	56.6	4.46
Change theory and change models, including change strategy, infrastructures and roles, change process, types of change, how people change, human reactions, pacing strategies, and impact analysis	0.0	0.5	6.9	29.0	63.6	4.56
Process thinking and design	0.0	2.3	12.1	43.3	42.3	4.26
Communication theory	0.0	3.7	17.2	40.0	39.1	4.14
Engagement practices to build critical mass	0.9	7.0	23.0	37.6	31.5	3.92
Diversity and inclusion, including managing difference	0.9	3.7	26.0	38.1	31.2	3.95
Motivation theory, including empowerment and rewards	0.0	3.7	15.4	42.5	38.3	4.15
Mindset/Mental models and their influence on behavior and performance	1.4	4.7	19.2	34.1	40.7	4.08

Key Actions: How important is each key action for effective performance in this professional area of expertise?

FACILITATING ORGANIZATIONAL CHANGE	Unnecessary	Slightly Important	Moderately Important	Very Important	Essential	Average
Establishes sponsorship and ownership for change	0.5	0.9	7.9	30.2	60.5	4.49
Creates a contract for change	0.0	2.8	14.9	35.3	47.0	4.27
Conducts diagnostic assessments	0.0	0.9	14.9	45.1	39.1	4.22
Provides feedback	0.0	0.0	5.1	38.6	56.3	4.51
Facilitates strategic planning for change	0.0	1.4	7.0	26.6	65.0	4.55
Builds involvement	0.0	0.5	4.7	31.6	63.3	4.58
Supports the change intervention	0.0	1.9	7.9	38.1	52.1	4.40
Integrates change into organizational culture	0.0	1.4	5.1	27.1	66.4	4.58
Manages consequences	0.0	1.9	13.1	36.6	48.4	4.31
Evaluates change results	0.0	2.4	9.4	43.9	44.3	4.30
Models mastery of leading change	0.0	2.4	8.5	30.7	58.5	4.45

Key Knowledge Areas: How important is each key knowledge area for effective performance in this professional area of expertise?

IMPROVING HUMAN PERFORMANCE	Unnecessary	Slightly Important	Moderately Important	Very Important	Essential	Average
Human performance improvement industry, including the mindset, vision, culture, and goals	0.0	4.6	24.1	41.7	29.6	3.96
Performance analysis and organizational analysis	0.0	0.9	8.3	37.8	53.0	4.43
Front-end analysis	0.0	0.9	12.9	36.4	49.8	4.35
Approaches for selecting performance-improvement solution	0.0	1.4	11.1	46.5	41.0	4.27
Change management theory	0.5	4.6	22.5	42.7	29.8	3.97
Measurement and evaluation methods and theory	0.5	0.5	20.3	42.9	35.9	4.13
Facilitation methods	0.9	0.5	18.4	41.0	39.2	4.17
Project management tools and techniques	0.5	1.8	24.3	46.8	26.6	3.97
Evaluation methods and theory	0.0	1.4	17.9	50.9	29.8	4.09
Communication channel, informal network, and alliance	0.0	0.9	16.1	39.4	43.6	4.26
Group dynamics process	0.0	1.8	19.7	39.9	38.5	4.15
Human Performance Improvement model	0.0	2.8	10.1	39.9	47.2	4.32
Systems thinking and theory	0.5	2.8	15.2	36.9	44.7	4.23
Questioning techniques	0.0	1.4	8.3	38.2	52.1	4.41

Key Actions: How important is each key action for effective performance in this professional area of expertise?

IMPROVING HUMAN PERFORMANCE	Unnecessary	Slightly Important	Moderately Important	Very Important	Essential	Average
Analyzes systems	0.0	2.3	14.6	43.2	39.9	4.21
Conducts performance analysis	0.0	0.5	4.2	38.1	57.2	4.52
Conducts cause analysis	0.0	1.9	4.7	37.7	55.8	4.47
Gathers data	0.0	0.9	11.6	45.4	42.1	4.29
Identifies the customer	0.0	0.9	7.4	37.5	54.2	4.45
Incorporates customer/stakeholder needs	0.0	0.9	6.5	33.3	59.3	4.51
Selects solutions	0.5	0.9	6.0	39.4	53.2	4.44
Manages and implements projects	0.5	2.3	14.9	49.8	32.6	4.12
Builds and sustains relationships	0.0	0.0	6.1	25.7	68.2	4.62
Evaluates results against organizational goals	0.0	1.4	7.4	36.1	55.1	4.45
Monitors change	0.0	1.9	10.8	47.4	39.9	4.25
Uses feedback skills	0.0	1.4	4.3	46.0	48.3	4.41

Key Knowledge Areas: How important is each key knowledge area for effective performance in this professional area of expertise?

MANAGING ORGANIZATIONAL KNOWLEDGE	Unnecessary	Slightly Important	Moderately Important	Very Important	Essential	Average
Knowledge management (KM) concepts, philosophy, and theory	0.0	2.5	15.2	49.4	32.9	4.13
Knowledge management history and best practices	0.0	9.1	23.4	53.2	14.3	3.73
Appreciation of the range of activities and initiatives used to establish an environment in which knowledge is effectively created, shared, and used to increase competitive advantage and customer satisfaction	0.0	2.6	11.7	48.1	37.7	4.21
Technology and how it enables the knowledge-sharing and learning process	0.0	2.6	15.6	42.9	39.0	4.18
Understanding of the primary processes of the business; experience with the organization's operations and business tools	0.0	0.0	13.0	29.9	57.1	4.44
Strategies and approaches to managing culture change	0.0	1.3	14.3	46.8	37.7	4.21
Information architecture	3.9	6.5	29.9	39.0	20.8	3.66
Database management	6.5	13.0	28.6	36.4	15.6	3.42
Business process analysis	0.0	3.9	21.1	38.2	36.8	4.08
Systems analysis and design	1.3	7.8	27.3	39.0	24.7	3.78
Adult learning theory	0.0	7.8	13.0	35.1	44.2	4.16
After Action Review (AAR) methodology	1.3	5.3	28.0	48.0	17.3	3.75

Key Actions: How important is each key action for effective performance in this professional area of expertise?

MANAGING ORGANIZATIONAL KNOWLEDGE	Unnecessary	Slightly Important	Moderately Important	Very Important	Essential	Average
Champions knowledge management (KM)	0.0	0.0	14.9	33.8	51.4	4.36
Benchmarks KM best practices and lessons learned	0.0	2.7	29.3	44.0	24.0	3.89
Creates a KM infrastructure	0.0	3.9	18.4	36.8	40.8	4.14
Leverages technology	0.0	1.3	22.4	39.5	36.8	4.12
Manages information life cycle	0.0	5.3	22.4	47.4	25.0	3.92
Encourages collaboration	0.0	1.3	13.3	28.0	57.3	4.41
Establishes a knowledge culture	0.0	1.3	11.8	28.9	57.9	4.43
Designs and implements KM solutions	0.0	0.0	22.4	46.1	31.6	4.09
Transforms knowledge into learning	0.0	0.0	9.3	33.3	57.3	4.48
Evaluates KM success	0.0	0.0	15.8	46.1	38.2	4.22

Key Knowledge Areas: How important is each key knowledge area for effective performance in this professional area of expertise?

MANAGING THE LEARNING FUNCTION	Unnecessary	Slightly Important	Moderately Important	Very Important	Essential	Average
Needs assessment methodologies and learning needs identification	0.0	1.3	7.9	42.3	48.5	4.38
Adult learning theory	0.0	2.1	16.3	39.6	42.1	4.22
Learning design theory	0.4	3.8	20.1	41.8	33.9	4.05
Learning technologies, such as distance learning, e-learning options	0.4	3.3	20.4	47.9	27.9	4.00
Learning information systems	0.4	7.5	32.1	44.6	15.4	3.67
Marketplace resources (that is, learning and performance products and services; capabilities of potential supplier partners)	0.8	8.8	31.8	41.0	17.6	3.66
Basic understanding of all learning, development, and performance programs being administered	0.0	2.1	14.2	41.0	42.7	4.24
Budgeting, accounting, and financial management	2.5	7.9	23.3	32.9	33.3	3.87
Principles of management	0.4	2.9	12.5	40.8	43.3	4.24
Project-planning tools and processes	0.0	4.6	21.3	47.5	26.7	3.96
Communication and influencing strategies and tools	0.0	0.0	5.4	37.2	57.3	4.52
Human resource systems and how they integrate, such as recruitment, selection, compensation, performance management, reward management	2.9	9.2	21.8	41.8	24.3	3.75
Organization's business model, drivers, and competitive position in the industry	0.0	6.7	20.5	36.0	36.8	4.03
External systems (that is, political, economic, sociological, cultural, and global factors that can affect the organization's performance in the marketplace)	3.3	12.5	36.7	32.1	15.4	3.44
Legal, regulatory, and ethical requirements pertaining to managing the learning function, such as federal/state/local employment laws like the ADA or EEOC Uniform Guidelines	2.9	10.4	22.5	37.5	26.7	3.75

Key Actions: How important is each key action for effective performance in this professional area of expertise?

MANAGING THE LEARNING FUNCTION	Unnecessary	Slightly Important	Moderately Important	Very Important	Essential	Average
Establishes a vision	0.0	1.7	7.9	31.0	59.4	4.48
Establishes strategies	0.0	0.8	4.2	31.7	63.3	4.58
Implements action plans	0.0	0.8	3.4	39.5	56.3	4.51
Develops and monitors the budget	2.9	7.5	15.0	38.8	35.8	3.97
Manages staff	2.5	3.3	10.9	31.4	51.9	4.27
Models leadership in developing people	1.3	1.7	5.0	35.0	57.1	4.45
Manages external resources	1.3	2.9	20.4	46.3	29.2	3.99
Ensures compliance with legal, ethical, and regulatory requirements	2.1	6.8	17.3	30.4	43.5	4.06

Key Knowledge Areas: How important is each key knowledge area for effective performance in this professional area of expertise?

MEASURING AND EVALUATING	Unnecessary	Slightly Important	Moderately Important	Very Important	Essential	Average
Statistical theory and methods	0.9	5.7	23.6	44.3	25.5	3.88
Research design	2.8	3.8	18.9	42.5	32.1	3.97
Analysis methods, such as cost-benefit analysis, return-on-investment, etc.	2.8	1.9	9.4	35.8	50.0	4.28
Interpretation and reporting of data	0.0	0.9	1.9	37.7	59.4	4.56
Theories and types of evaluation, such as the four levels of evaluation	1.0	3.8	10.5	33.3	51.4	4.30

Key Actions: How important is each key action for effective performance in this professional area of expertise?

MEASURING AND EVALUATING	Unnecessary	Slightly Important	Moderately Important	Very Important	Essential	Average
Identifies customer expectations	1.0	1.9	3.9	36.9	56.3	4.46
Selects appropriate strategies, research design, and measures	0.0	1.0	8.7	43.3	47.1	4.37
Communicates and gains support for the measurement and evaluation plan	0.0	2.9	10.6	37.5	49.0	4.33
Manages data collection	0.0	0.0	11.5	52.9	35.6	4.24
Analyzes and interprets data	0.0	0.0	3.8	34.6	61.5	4.58
Reports conclusions and makes recommendations based on finding	0.0	0.0	0.0	27.9	72.1	4.72

What percentage of the knowledge, skills, and abilities that are needed for effective performance of your job were covered by the roles, general competencies, and professional areas of expertise appearing in this survey?

Percent Coverage	Percent Selected
0%	0.1%
5%	0.1%
10%	0.1%
15%	0.3%
20%	0.2%
25%	0.4%
30%	0.6%
35%	0.2%
40%	0.2%
45%	0.1%
50%	1.2%
55%	0.4%
60%	1.4%
65%	0.9%
70%	4.3%
75%	7.0%
80%	9.8%
85%	9.6%
90%	20.3%
95%	16.5%
100%	26.3%

How important do you believe the following factors will be to the workplace learning and performance profession over the next three years?

	Unnecessary	Slightly Important	Moderately Important	Very Important	Essential	N/A	Average
Aligning learning and performance strategies with the organization's strategy	0.1	0.7	4.9	25.1	68.5	0.7	4.62
Demonstrating a payback from your efforts in the form of improved organizational performance and measurable results	0.3	1.9	11.8	36.9	48.1	1.0	4.32
Operating ethically and with social responsibility	0.2	1.6	12.8	29.4	54.3	1.7	4.38
Developing or offering learning tools to meet the need for just-in-time learning and knowledge	0.2	2.0	13.2	40.5	42.3	1.9	4.25
Understanding and responding to globalization and diversity issues	1.5	7.7	27.4	37.1	23.9	2.3	3.76
Developing and implementing strategies for retaining and developing talent	0.4	2.6	13.6	35.5	45.3	2.8	4.26
Increasing competence in understanding technology alternatives and their use and application in delivering learning and training	0.6	3.1	16.9	37.9	39.2	2.3	4.15

Appendix E

Project Contributors

Individual Contributors

ASTD, DDI, and Rothwell & Associates want to acknowledge the people, organizations, and ASTD chapters listed on the following pages as well as all others whose help and input contributed to this study. The authors greatly appreciate their efforts.

Joerg Abramowski
Senior Manager
Audi Academy
Beijing, China

Linda Ackerman Anderson
Co-Founder and Vice President
Being First Inc.
Durango, CO

Jill Allemang
Graduate Student
Northwestern University
Evanston, IL

Mark Allen
President and Chief Executive
    Officer
Corporate University Xchange
    Inc.
New York, NY

Andrew M. Amalfitano
Director, Global Learning
    Solutions
Storage Technology Corporation
Louisville, CO

Debra M. Amidon
Founder and Chief Executive
    Officer
Entovation International Ltd.
Wilmington, MA

Heather Annulis
Assistant Professor
University of Southern Mississippi
Hattiesburg, MS

Jean Avison
Learning and Development
    Consultant
Wells Fargo
Portland, OR

Jeanne Baer
President
Creative Training Solutions
Lincoln, NE

Jean Barbazette
President
The Training Clinic
Seal Beach, CA

Laura Barnett
Marketing Manager
PWPL
Tucson, AZ

Barbara K. Beach
Executive Director
Management Concepts Inc.
Vienna, VA

Maretha Behrens
Change and Development
    Consultant
Relationship Manager
Deloitte & Touche Human
    Capital Corp.

Joseph A. Benkowski
Associate Dean for Outreach
Director STTI
University of Wisconsin-Stout
Menomonie, WI

Maureen Betses
Vice President
Higher Education and eLearning
Deputy for Training and
    Development
Harvard Business School
Boston, MA

Elaine Biech
President
ebb associates inc
Virginia Beach, VA

Peter Block
Partner
Designed Learning
West Mystic, CT

Dianna Booher
President and Chief Executive
  Officer
Booher Consultants
Dallas, TX

John Bott
Manager of Education
Dana University
Louisville, KY

Phil Braden
Tropicana
Bradenton, FL

Mary L. Broad
Principal
Performance Excellence
Chevy Chase, MD

Veronica Bruhl
Maple Park, IL

Jean Broom
Executive Director of Human
  Resources
Estee Lauder
New York, NY

Laura Bunte

W. Warner Burke
Edward Lee Thorndike
Professor of Psychology and
  Education
Program Coordinator, Graduate
  Programs in Social-
  Organizational Psychology
Teachers College, Columbia
  University
New York, NY

Holly Burkett
Principal
Evaluation Works
Davis, CA

Bill Byham
Chairman and Chief Executive
  Officer
DDI
Bridgeville, PA

Molly Byock
Management Trainee Training
  Supervisor
University of Toyota Motor Sales,
  U.S.A. Inc.
Torrance, CA

Steve Callender
Wilson Learning
Eden Prairie, MN

Kay Cannon
At-Large Director
International Coaching Federation
Lexington, KY

Todd Cash
Operations Training Manager
Praxair Inc.
Tonawanda, NY

Richard V. Chang
Chief Executive Officer
Richard Chang Associates Inc.
Irvine, CA

Janet Cherry
Training Advisor
FedEx Corporation
Memphis, TN

Kathryn Collins
Director, Worldwide Training
  and Organization Effectiveness
Texas Instruments
Dallas, TX

Pat Crull
Vice President and Chief
  Learning Officer
Toys "R" Us
Wayne, NJ

Joe DiStefano
Professor
International Institute for
  Management Development
Switzerland

Margaret Driscoll
Manager
IBM Lotus Mindspan Solutions
Cambridge, MA

Mary Eckenrod
Director, Executive Development
Cisco Systems Inc.
San Jose, CA

Paul Elliott
Saba Software Inc.
Redwood City, CA

Sharon Epstein
President
Next Level Development Inc.
Plano, TX

Judy Estrin
President
Partners In Enterprise Inc.
Burbank, CA

Colleen Fahy
Senior Consultant
Booz Allen Hamilton
NJ

Wendy Ferguson
Regional Management Trainer
Geico
San Diego, CA

Adolpho Fernandes, Jr.
Manager
Senac Rio
Brazil

Jennifer Foil
Research Associate
University of Southern Mississippi
Hattiesburg, MS

Stacy Fortress
Supervisor, Quality Assurance
   and Training
Overland Park, KS

Elena Galbraith
Performance Improvement
   Program Manager
Microsoft Corporation
Redmond, WA

Cyndi Gaudet
Director
Workplace Learning and
   Performance Center
University of Southern Mississippi
Hattiesburg, MS

Gloria Gery
President
Gery Associates
Tolland, MA

Cheryl Getzan
Project Leader
Tropicana
Bradenton, FL

Nancy Giese
Performance Improvement
   Consultant
Director of Learning and
   Development
The Working Force

Christie Gilbert
Director of Global Learning
   and Development
Memec
San Diego, CA

David Gurteen
President
Gurteen Associates
United Kingdom

Judith A. Hale
President
Hale Associates
Downers Grove, IL

Elizabeth Hannah
Manager, HPI Certificate Program
ASTD
Alexandria, VA

Mike Hansen
Senior Vice President
Veridian Corporation
Arlington, VA

Phil Harkins
President
Linkage Incorporated
Lexington, MA

Darin Hartley
LGuide
Seattle, WA

James A. Haudan
President and Chief Executive
   Officer
Root Learning Inc.
Maumee, OH

Cindy Heck
Training Manager
Astra Zeneca

Sidney Henkin
Prism Learning Solutions
Farmington Hills, MI

Ann Herrmann-Nehdi
Chief Executive Officer
Herrmann International
Lake Lure, NC

Diane Hessan
President and Chief Executive
   Officer
Communispace Corporation
Watertown, MA

Blanco High
Program Consultant
U.S. Dept. of Veterans Affairs
Washington, DC

Katherine Holt
President
Peakinsight LLC
Durango, CO

Dmitri Hong
Project Manager
Korean Management Association
Seoul, South Korea

Janis S. Houston
Principal Research Scientist
Personnel Decisions Research
   Institutes Inc.
Minneapolis, MN

Cindy Huggett
Learning and Development
   Manager
Kinetic Systems Inc.
Durham, NC

John Humphrey
Chairman
Humphrey Enterprises LLC
Boston, MA

Ronald Jacobs
Professor
Workforce Development and
    Education
Ohio State University
Columbus, OH

Al Jesness
Senior Director of Training
Allied DomecqQSR
Randolph, MA

Jerry Kaminski
Senior Training Coordinator
American Axle & Manufacturing
Grosse Pointe Park, MI

Judy Katz
Executive Vice President
The Kaleel Jamsion Consulting
    Group
Troy, NY

Beverly Kaye
Founder/Chief Executive Officer
Career Systems
Sherman Oaks, CA

Ron Kempf
Director, Project Management,
    Competency, and Certification
HP Services
Livonia, MI

Lisa Kimball
Executive Director
Group Jazz
Washington, DC

Bill Kline
Vice President, Human Resources,
Marketing, and Chief Learning
    Officer
Delta Air Lines
Atlanta, GA

Deirdre Knapp
Manager
Assessment Research and Analysis
    Program
Human Resources Research
    Organization
Alexandria, VA

Jesse Kramer
Instructional Designer
Ewing, NJ

Margaret Krigbaum
Vice President
International Coaching Federation
Tucson, AZ

Tom LaBonte
Managing Director
Workplace Performance LLC
Huntersville, NC

Linda E. Laddin
Managing Director
Wise Resources Limited
Hong Kong, China

Se-Kwang Lee
Consultant
Global Management Institute
Seoul, South Korea

Teresa Lubeck
Manager Content Development
Lucent Technologies

Noreen MacMahon
Verona, NJ

Victor L. Magdaraog
SGV-DDI
Philippines

Richard Marcus
Managing Consultant
Manchester
Horsham, PA

Michael Marquardt
Professor
George Washington University
Washington, DC

Helene Martins de Araujo
Trinamento & Desenvolvimento
Brazil

Jane Massy
Consultant
Cambridge, United Kingdom

Catherine Mattiske
President
The Performance Company
    Pty Ltd.
NSW, Australia

June Maul
Chief Learning Officer
Advantage Value LLC
Scottsdale, AZ

Lee Maxey
Vice President
Professional Services and Alliances
Five Star Development Inc.
Duxbury, MA

Debra McKinney Gehman
Director of Corporate University
Bolivar, Colombia

Suzanne McCullagh
Education Services Coordinator
CSTD
Toronto, Canada

Pat McLagan
President and Chief Executive
  Officer
The RITEstuff Inc.
and McLagan International Inc.
Washington, DC

Donna McNamara
Vice President
Global Education and Training
Colgate Palmolive Co.
New York, NY

Kevin H. McNamara
Vice President, Global Training
Allied DomecqQSR
Randolf, MA

Zandile Mcutshenge
Senior Manager
South African Post Office
Pretoria, South Africa

Bill Meal
Consultant
Dennison Consulting
Ann Arbor, MI

Jeanne Meister
Independent Consultant
New York, NY

Gary C. Miller
Director of HR Services
AIPSO
Ontario, Canada

Bernice Moore
Project Manager
CTB/McGraw-Hill
New York, NY

Eli Munzer
Chief eLearning Architect
Verizon Communications
Tampa, FL

Nancy Nagle
Director
Retailer Education and Training
Ford Motor Company
Dearborn, MI

Priscilla D. Nelson
Principal/Lead Consultant
Nelson & Associates
Reston, VA

William J. Nijhof
Professor in Education
University Twente
Enschede, The Netherlands

Kevin Oakes
Chairman and Chief Executive
  Officer
Click2learn
Bellevue, WA

Gary O'Dell
Performance Consultant
Cox Communications
Rancho Santa Margarita, CA

Julio Olalla
Founder
The Newfield Network Inc.
Olney, MD

Julie O'Mara
President
O'Mara and Associates
Castro Valley, CA

Stefan Oppitz
Consultant
A-M-T Management
  Performance AG
Radevormwald, Germany

Germán A. Paris
President
P&B
Colombia

Warren Payne
Training Specialist
EMC Mortgage
Irving, TX

George Phelps
Director Business Development
MAPSLawrence Tech
  University
Southfield, MI

Jack Phillips
Executive Vice President
Jack Phillips Center for Research
Chelsea, AL

Nancy Piatt
Vice President
Learning and Development
Thomson Learning
Voorheesville, NY

Steve Piersanti
President
Berrett-Koehler
San Francisco, CA

Dana Pitts
Compliance Training Specialist
Alcon
Fort Worth, TX

Howard Pratt
Vice President
Learning and Development
Jantoh, Block & Rathbone
Cleveland, OH

Sandy J. Price
Vice President
Human Resources Development
Sprint
Overland Park, KS

Donnee Ramelli
President
General Motors University
Detroit, MI

Nancy Randa
Deputy Associate Director for
    Talent
United States Office of Personnel
    Management
Washington, DC

Rebecca Ray
President
Comcast University
New York, NY

Richard Redden
Learning Consultant
Manager, Internal Training and
    Development
Learn Stream
New Brunswick, NJ

Cathy Rezak
President
Paradigm Learning
Tampa, FL

Greg Rider
Training Manager
New York, NY

T. Randall Riggs
Senior Human Resource Manager
Agere Systems
Macungie, PA

Marilee Robertson
Interactive Training Design
Phoenix, AZ

Dana Robinson
President
Partners in Change Inc.
Pittsburgh, PA

Jim Robinson
President
Partners in Change Inc.
Pittsburgh, PA

Marc Rosenberg
Consultant
Mark Rosenberg and Associates
Hillsborough, NJ

Allison Rossett
Professor of Educational
    Technology
San Diego State University
San Diego, CA

Ethan S. Sanders
President and Chief Executive
    Officer
Sundial Learning Systems Inc.
Alexandria, VA

Edward E. Scannell
Director
Center for Professional
    Development
    & Training
Scottsdale, AZ

Kathy Schramek
Director of Programs and
    Certifications
International Coach Federation
Washington, DC

Lynn Schmidt
Director, Leadership Institute
Nextel Communications
Reston, VA

Peter Senge
Chairperson
Center for Organizational
    Learning
Sloan School of Management,
    MIT
Cambridge, MA

Daryl Sink
Chief Executive Officer
Daryl Sink Associates
Monterey, CA

Shelley Siu
President
Shelley Siu International
Singapore

Martyn Sloman
Advisor
Learning, Training, and
    Development
CIPD
London, United Kingdom

Harold D. Stolovitch
Principal
HSA Learning & Performance
    Solutions
Los Angeles, CA

Bonita Stoufer
Managing Director, Learning
    Service Organization
Delta Air Lines
Atlanta, GA

Brenda Sugrue
Director of Research
ASTD
Alexandria, VA

Clifton Taulbert
President
The Building Community
    Institute
Tulsa, OK

Evert Temminck
General Manager
DDI
The Netherlands

Lita Theron
Training Consultant
South African Breweries

Nancy Thomas
Director
The Chauncey Group
   International
a Division of Capstar
Princeton, NJ

Tina Tipps
Curriculum Development Team
   Leader
Toyota
Newport Beach, CA

Rochelle Tros
Project Manager Finance
   Academy
Unilieve
London, United Kingdom

Anthony Twigger
Executive Director
IFTDO
Geneva, Switzerland

Marty Val Hill
President
Professional Developments
Pleasant Grove, UT

Mark E. Van Buren
Strategic Research Consultant
Corporate Executive Board
Washington, DC

Karen Vander Linde
Partner
PricewaterhouseCoopers
McLean, VA

Christian Voelkl
Senior Consultant
E&E Info Consultants
Berlin, Germany

Min Jaun Wang
Assistant Professor
San Diego State University
San Diego, CA

Brad Ward
Executive Director
Neflin
Orange Park, FL

Linda Waters
Managing Principal
The Chauncey Group
   International
a Division of Capstar
Princeton, NJ

Margaret Wheatley
President
The Berkana Institute
Provo, UT

Ben Whitley
HR Representative
Enogex
Oklahoma City, OK

Laura Whitworth
Co-Founder
The Coaches Training Institute
Sebastopol, CA

Sharon Wingron
Leadership Consultant
Wings of Success LLC
St. Louis, MO

Jack Zenger
Vice President
Novations
Midway, UT

Chet Zoltak
CLO
Towers Perrin Administration
   Solutions
Philadelphia, PA

Participating Organizations

AITD

Australian Institute of Training
   and Development
West Chatswood
New South Wales
Australia
http://www.aitd.com.au/

CLO Magazine

Chicago, IL
www.clomedia.com

CSTD

Canadian Society for Training
   and Development
Toronto, Ontario
Canada
www.cstd.ca

IFTDO

International Federation of
   Training and Development
   Organisations
Geneva, Switzerland
www.iftdo.org

NVO2

Dutch association of HRD
   professionals
Apeldoorn, The Netherlands
www.nvvo.nl

Participating ASTD Chapters

Cascadia Chapter
Beaverton, OR

Central Iowa Chapter
West Des Moines, IA

Chicago Chapter
Chicago, IL

Detroit Chapter
Bloomfield Hills, MI

Genesee Valley Chapter
Rochester, NY

Greater Philadelphia Chapter
Wayne, PA

Lincoln Chapter
Lincoln, NE

New York Metro Chapter
New York, NY

Northwest Wisconsin Chapter
Eau Claire, WI

Omaha Chapter
Omaha, NE

Roanoke Chapter
Roanoke, VA

San Diego Chapter
San Diego, CA

Southeast Wisconsin Chapter
Pewaukee, WI

These chapters circulated invitations to encourage member participation. Individual members from chapters not listed above also contributed to the survey.

Summit Participants

Paul R. Bernthal
Manager
Center for Applied Behavioral
   Research (CABER)
DDI
Bridgeville, PA

Bill Byham
Chairman and Chief Executive
   Officer
DDI
Bridgeville, PA

Karen Colteryahn
Manager
Knowledge Management
DDI
Bridgeville, PA

Patty Davis
DDI Competency Project
Manager
Senior Consultant
DDI
Longboat Key, FL

Judith A. Hale
President
Hale Associates
Downers Grove, IL

Janis S. Houston
Principal Research Scientist
Personnel Decisions Research
   Institutes Inc.
Minneapolis, MN

Jennifer Naughton
Competency Project Manager
ASTD
Alexandria, VA

Doug Reynolds
Manager, Assessment Technology
   Group
DDI
Bridgeville, PA

Sheryl Riddle
Senior Vice President
Consulting and Client Delivery
DDI
Bridgeville, PA

William J. Rothwell
President
Rothwell & Associates Inc.
State College, PA

Paula Steinhauser
Project Associate
DDI
Bridgeville, PA

Deborah Jo King Stern
Ph.D. Intern
Workforce Education and
   Development
College of Education,
   Department of Learning and
   Performance Systems
The Pennsylvania State University
University Park, PA

Nancy Thomas
Director
The Chauncey Group
   International
a Division of Capstar
Princeton, NJ

Rich Wellins
Senior Vice President of Global
   Marketing
DDI
Bridgeville, PA

References

Aldrich, C. (2003). "Global learning, 2008." In George M. Piskurich (Ed.), *The AMA handbook of e-learning: Effective design, implementation, and technology solutions.* New York: AMACOM.

Aldrich, C. (2003). *Simulations and the future of learning: An innovative (and perhaps revolutionary) approach to e-learning.* San Francisco: Pfeiffer.

Ante, S.E. (2003, June 23). "Savings tip: Don't do it yourself." *Business Week, 3838,* 78–79.

Bauer, L., Heinl, R., & McGovern, C. (2003, June). *Consultant competency model role-based analysis.* Pittsburgh, PA: Development Dimensions International.

Bennis, W., Burke, W.W., Gery, G., Juechter, W.M., Rummler, G., & Tichy, N. (2003, January). "What lies ahead." *T+D, 57*(1), 32–43.

Bernstein, R., & Bergman, M. (2003, June 18). "Hispanic population reaches all-time high of 38.8 million, new Census Bureau estimates show." U.S. Census Bureau/United States Department of Commerce. Retrieved from http://www.census.gov/Press-Release /www/2003/cb03-100.html.

Bernthal, P.R., & Wellins, R.S. (2003). *Leadership forecast: A benchmarking study.* Pittsburgh, PA: Development Dimensions International.

Bierema, L.L., Bing, J.W., & Carter, T.J. (2002, May). "The global pendulum." *T+D, 56*(5), 70–78.

Brewster, C., Farndale, E., & van Ommeren, J. (2000, June). "HR competencies and professional standards." World Federation of Personnel Management Associations. Retrieved from http://www.wfpma .com/comp.pdf.

Brewster, C., Farndale, E., & Whittaker, J. (2000, July). "Skills, knowledge and professional HR standards." *WORLDLINK, 10*(3), 4–5. Retrieved from http://www.wfpma.com/PDFs/wlv10n3.pdf.

Brockbank, W., & Ulrich, D. (2003). *The human resource competency toolkit* [includes *Competencies for the new HR* guidebook and online assessment]. Alexandria, VA: Society for Human Resource Management, University of Michigan Business School, Global Consulting Alliance.

Catano, V. (1998, April). "Appendix 1: Competencies: A review of the literature and bibliography." Canadian Council of Human Resources Associations/Conseil canadien des associations en ressources humaines (CCHRA/CCARH). Retrieved from http://www .cchra-ccarh.ca/en/phaseIreport/bibliography.asp.

Caudron, S. (2003, January). "HR is dead . . . Long live HR." *Workforce, 82*(1), 26–30.

The Change Strategist Workshop [organizational change workshop for leaders]. (1998). Pittsburgh, PA: Development Dimensions International.

Cole, C., Gale, S., Greengard, S., Kiger, P., Lachnitt, C., Raphael, T., Shuit, D., & Wiscombe, J. (2003, June). "Fast forward: 25 trends that will change the way you do business." *Workforce, 82*(6), 43–44, 46, 48–56.

DiStefano, J. (1999). *Generic competency dictionary for general management roles.* Hong Kong: Hong Kong Productivity Council.

Dixon, V., Conway, K., Ashley, K., & Stewart, N. (2001). *Training competency architecture* (2d ed.). Toronto, ON: Ontario Society for Training and Development.

Drickhamer, D. (2002, March). "Medical marvel: From order to invoice, Siemens Computed Tomography optimizes total logistics to serve its customers." *IndustryWeek, 251*(3), 47–49.

Foshay, W., Silber, K., & Westgaard, O. (1986). *Instructional design competencies: The standards.* Iowa City, IA: International Board of Standards for Training, Performance and Instruction.

Foshay, W., Silber, K., & Westgaard, O. (1990). *Training manager competencies: The standards.* Iowa City, IA: International Board of Standards for Training, Performance and Instruction.

Foxon, M., Richey, R.C., Roberts, R., & Spannaus, T. (2003). *Training manager competencies: The standards* (2d ed.). Syracuse, NY: ERIC Clearinghouse on Information & Technology.

French, H.W. (2003, July 24). "Insular Japan needs, but resists, immigration." *The New York Times,* (52554), A1.

Galvin, T., Johnson, G., & Barbian, J. (2003, March). "The 2003 *Training* top 100." *Training, 40*(3), 18.

Gilley, J.W., & Galbraith, M.W. (1986, June). "Examining professional certification." *Training and Development Journal, 40*(6), 60–61.

Gilley, J.W., Quatro, S.A., & Lynham, S.A. (2002). "Strategic HRD and its transformation." In A.M. Gilley, J.L. Callahan, & L.L. Bierema (Eds.), *Critical issues in HRD: A new agenda for the twenty-first century,* 23–48. Cambridge, MA: Perseus Publishing.

Girmm, D. (2001, April). "What's keeping global corporations awake at night? It's no longer business as usual." *CMA Management, 75*(2), 52–53.

"Global HR 'competencies' project gets under way." (1998, October). *WORLDLINK,* 1. Retrieved from http://www.wfpma.com/PDFs/wloct98.pdf.

Goodyear, P., Salmon, G., Spector, M., Steeples, C., & Tickner, S. (2001). "Competencies for online teaching." *Educational Technology Research and Development, 49*(1), 65.

Hale, J. (2000). *Performance-based certification: How to design a valid, defensible, cost-effective program.* San Francisco: Jossey-Bass/Pfeiffer.

Harris, P. (2003, September). "Outsourced learning: A new market." *T+D, 57*(9), 30–38.

Hutchison, C., Shepherd, J., & Stein, F. (1988). *Instructor competencies: The standards (Vol. I).* Batavia, NY: International Board of Standards for Training, Performance and Instruction.

International Board of Standards for Training, Performance and Instruction. (1986). *Instructional design competencies: The standards.* Batavia, IL: Author.

International Board of Standards for Training, Performance and Instruction. (1993). *Instructor competencies: The standards—Vol 1 and Vol. 2.* Batavia, IL: Author.

International Board of Standards for Training, Performance and Instruction. (1994). *Instructional design competencies: The standards* (2d ed.). Batavia, IL: Author.

International Board of Standards for Training, Performance and Instruction. (2003). *Instructor competencies.* Retrieved http://www.ibstpi.org /Instructor_Competencies.htm

Jackson, T. (2002, Winter). "The management of people across cultures: Valuing people differently." *Human Resource Management, 41*(4), 455–475.

Jamrog, J.J. (2002). "Current practices: The coming decade of the employee, HR." *Human Resource Planning, 25*(3), 5–11.

Kemske, F. (1998, January). "HR 2008: A forecast based on our exclusive study." *Workforce, 77*(1), 47–60.

Leonard, B. (1998). "HRCI celebrates a 25th anniversary." *HRMagazine, 43*(3), 101–102.

May, G.L., & Kahnweiler, B. (2002, July). "Shareholder value: Is there common ground?" *T+D, 56*(7), 45–52.

McClenahen, J.S. (2003, October). "Lean and teams: More than blips." *IndustryWeek, 252*(10), 63–64.

McLagan, P. (1989). *Models for HRD practice* [4 volumes]. Alexandria, VA: ASTD.

McLagan, P.A. (2002, November–2003, February). Change Leadership series [Nov.: "Change leadership today," pp. 26–31; Dec.: "Success with change," pp. 44–53; Jan.: "The change-capable organization," pp. 50–58; Feb.: "Distributed intelligence," pp. 52–56]. *T+D, 56*(11), *56*(12), *57*(1), *57*(2).

McLagan, P., & McCullough, R. (1983). *Models for excellence: The conclusions and recommendations of the ASTD training and development competency study.* Alexandria, VA: ASTD.

Patel, D. (2002, July). *SHRM® workplace forecast: A strategic outlook 2002–2003*. Alexandria, VA: Society for Human Resource Management.

Pinto, P., & Walker, J. (1978). *A study of professional training and development roles and competencies*. Madison, WI: ASTD.

Piskurich, G.M., & Sanders, E.S. (1998). *ASTD models for learning technologies: Roles, competencies, and outputs*. Alexandria, VA: ASTD.

Reed, S.O. (2002, May/June). "The new organization and implications for training." *Performance Improvement Journal, 41*(5), 24–28.

Richey, R.C., Fields, D.C., & Foxon, M., with Roberts, R.C., Spannaus, T., & Spector, J.M. (2001). *Instructional design competencies: The standards* (3d ed.) [ED453803]. (Available from the Educational Resources Information Center (ERIC) database at http://www.eric.ed.gov/)

Rivera, C.T. (2002, November 1). "Office 2005: Trends to watch in the next three years." *OfficeSolutions, 19*(9), 12–14.

Rogers, R.W., & Riddle, S. (2003). *Trust in the workplace* (Monograph). Pittsburgh, PA: Development Dimensions International.

Roper Starch Worldwide. (1999, February). "Baby boomers envision their retirement: An AARP segmentation analysis." American Association of Retired Persons. Retrieved from http://research.aarp.org/econ/boomer_seg.html.

Rothwell, W. (1996). *ASTD models for human performance improvement: Roles, competencies, and outputs*. Alexandria, VA: ASTD.

Rothwell, W. (Ed.). (2000). *ASTD models for human performance improvement* (2d ed.). Alexandria, VA: ASTD.

Rothwell, W.J., Sanders, E.S., & Soper, J.G. (1999). *ASTD models for workplace learning and performance: Roles, competencies, outputs*. Alexandria, VA: ASTD.

Rothwell, W.J., & Sredl, H.J. (2000). *The ASTD reference guide to workplace learning and performance: Present and future roles and competencies* (3d ed.). Amherst, MA: Human Resource Development Press.

Ruona, W.E.A. (in press). *What's in a name? Human resource development and its core*. Athens, GA: University of Georgia.

Salopek, J.L. (2003, March). "The new MBA for trainers." *T+D, 57*(3), 71–73.

Spector, J.M., & de la Teja, I. (2001, December). *Competencies for online teaching* [EDO-IR-2001-09]. (Available from the Educational Resources Information Center (ERIC) database at http://www.eric.ed.gov/)

Strategic Leadership Experience [four-day simulation experience for senior-level leaders]. (2001). Pittsburgh, PA: Development Dimensions International.

Sunoo, B.P. (1999, May). "HR education: So . . . where to begin?" *Workforce, 78*(5), 76.

Sunoo, B.P. (1999, May). "Specialized certificates offered to HR." *Workforce, 78*(5), 74.

Task Force on Assessment Center Standards. (1979). "Standards and ethical considerations for assessment center operations." *Journal of Assessment Center Technology, 2*(2).

Taylor, C.R. (October, 2002). "E-learning: The second wave." *T+D, 56*(10), 24–31.

Thompson, C., Koon, E., Woodwell, W.H., Jr., & Beauvais, J. (2002, December). *Training for the next economy: An ASTD state of the industry report on trends in employer-provided training in the United States*. Alexandria, VA: ASTD.

Thottam, J. (2003, August 4). "Where the good jobs are going." *Time, 162*(5), 36–38.

U.S. General Accounting Office. (2001). "Older workers: Demographic trends pose challenges for employers and workers." Washington, DC: Author. Retrieved from http://www.gao.gov/new.items/d0285.pdf.

Van Buren, M.E., & Erskine, W. (2002, February). *State of the industry report*. Alexandria, VA: ASTD.

Walker, J.W. (2002). "Perspectives, HR." *Human Resource Planning, 25*(1), 12–14.

"WFPMA research findings." (2000, January). *WORLDLINK, 10*(1), 1. Retrieved from http://www.wfpma.com/PDFs/wlv10n1.pdf.

"What's ahead for HR? SHRM research identifies top trends." (2002). *HRfocus, 79*(9), 8–9.

Whittaker, J. (1998, October). "Towards global standards." *WORLDLINK,* 4–5. Retrieved from http://www.wfpma.com/PDFs/wloct98.pdf.

Whittaker, J. (2000, January). "What is an HR professional?" *WORLDLINK, 10*(1), 6–7. Retrieved from http://www.wfpma.com/PDFs/wlv10n1.pdf.

Wiley, C. (1992, August). "The certified HR professional." *HRMagazine, 37*(8), 77.

Wilhelm, W.R. (1995, Summer). "Response to 'reexamining professional certification in human resource management,' by Carolyn Wiley." *Human Resource Management, 34*(2), 295.

World Future Society. (2003). *Top 10 forecasts from Outlook 2003.* Retrieved from http://www.wfs.org/forecasts.htm.

Zahn, D. (2001, April). "Training: A function, profession, calling, what?" *T+D, 55*(4), 36–41.

Websites

Following is a partial listing of Web sites referenced in producing this report:

American Society for Training and Development (ASTD): http://www.astd.org

Australian Institute of Training and Development (AITD): http://www.aitd.com.au

Canadian Council of Human Resources Associations/Conseil canadien des associations en ressources humaines (CCHRA-CCARH): http://www.cchra-ccarh.ca

Canadian Society for Training and Development (CSTD): http://www.cstd.ca

Chartered Institute of Personnel and Development (CIPD): http://www.cipd.co.uk

Human Resource Certification Institute (HRCI): http://www.hrci.org

International Board of Standards for Training, Performance and Instruction (ibstpi): http://www.ibstpi.org

International Coach Federation (ICF): http://www.coachfederation.org

International Federation of Training and Development Organisations (IFTDO): http://www.iftdo.org

International Society for Performance Improvement (ISPI): http://www.ispi.org

Organization Development Institute (OD Institute): http://www.members.aol.com/odinst/index.htm

Organization Development Network (ODN): http://www.odnetwork.org

Professional Assessment Resources Center (PARC)/Centre de ressources pour l'évaluation (CRE) of the Canadian Council of Human Resources Associations/Conseil canadien des associations en ressources humaines (CCHRA/CCARH): http://www.cchra-ccarh.ca/parc/default.htm

Society for Human Resource Management (SHRM): http://www.shrm.org

World Federation of Personnel Management Associations (WFPMA): http://www.wfpma.com

WorldatWork: http://www.worldatwork.org